BRINGING SONS INTO GLORY
INTO GLORY
and
MAKING
ALL THINGS
NEW

Discovery House
PUBLISHERS
BOX 3566 · GRAND RAPIDS, MI 49501

*PUBLISHING BOOKS THAT FEED
THE SOUL WITH THE WORD OF GOD.*

CHRISTIAN LITERATURE CRUSADE
Fort Washington, Pennsylvania 19034

BRINGING SONS INTO GLORY
and
MAKING ALL THINGS NEW

OSWALD CHAMBERS

*Published through special arrangement with the
Oswald Chambers Publications Association*

CONTENTS

Contents continued

Foreword to Previous Editions

I have rough notes of these lectures as given in their first form at the Perth Convention in 1914. I sat enthralled at the beauty and power of the truth being given to us. The essential message of this book was expressed then in these words: "In the life of our Lord, as Son of Man, when He transformed innocence into holiness by a series of moral choices, He gave the pattern forever of how a holy character was to be developed." It is a basic book. It reminds me of Henry Scougal's *Life of God in the Soul of Man,* a volume that greatly influenced Whitfield and the Wesleys. That Aberdeen Professor wrote in 1668, "The power and life of religion may be better expressed in actions than in words. . . . They are perfectly exemplified in the Holy life of our blessed Savior, a main part of whose business in this world was to teach by His practice what He did require of others; and to make His own conversation an exact resemblance of those rules which He prescribed. So that if ever true goodness was visible to mortal eyes it was then when His presence did beautify and illustrate this lower world."

Oswald Chambers here shows us the parallel between our Lord's wondrous life on earth and our life lived in His Name. The psychology of the sanctified life is perfectly illustrated in our Lord's life as set forth in the gospels. The First Adam mishandled and disarranged his human nature. The Last Adam restored human nature to a right working relation to God. When through the atonement and the new birth we are lifted into the shared life of our risen Lord, the same laws of development operate for us as with Him. And "Christian psychology is not a knowledge of man, but a knowledge of our Lord Jesus Christ." To profit by this book demands concentrated thought, with Bible in hand, and with a humble eagerness to "act on the Word, instead of merely listening to it and deluding yourselves" (James 1:22 Moffat). This book shows how "holiness" works out in human nature as we know it. It shows how sin has taken possession of human nature, but that sin is abnormal. Sin is the outcome of a relationship which God never ordained. Our Lord in His human nature cancelled that wrong relationship through His cross and established a new relationship. It is in that new relationship we work out that holiness of life and thought and feeling and purpose and service which is the fulfillment of the New Covenant promise (Hebrews 8:10-12).

It is required of us that we walk even as He walked. Jesus Christ is the firstborn of many brethren, the Elder Brother of a vast family of brothers, and it is our privilege to bear the family likeness of Jesus Christ. In Him we see the Son of God—the exact expression of Almighty God; and also the Son of Man—the presentation of God's normal man. At times Jesus Christ lifts the veil from His own consciousness and we are permitted to gaze with awe into the depths of that sacred personality. But the end is to be that we become partakers of the Divine nature, and build up ourselves in our most holy faith, and so grow up into Him in all things, who is the Head, even Christ.

I pray that the book may prove as great a blessing to many thoughtful students as it has been to some of us for years, bringing them to the apostolic climax of confession, "For to me to live IS CHRIST."

David Lambert

Publisher's Foreword

The focus of the life and ministry of Oswald Chambers was on the person and work of Jesus Christ. His passion for our Lord and the truth of His indwelling the believer is clearly the dominant theme of Chambers' writings, but it is in this combined volume that we see this motif played in concert with the major events of the life of Christ. The writer is never content to leave us with the facts of the historical event, nor with the truth as it relates to Christ Himself, but also proceeds to relate this marvelous subject to the believer—making real the life of Christ in and through us by virtue of our spiritual union with Him.

Discovery House Publishers is pleased to introduce this new edition of these two titles, revised and combined into one volume. The titles by the page numbers indicate from which book that chapter comes. Our thanks to Arthur Neil, the editor of The Oswald Chambers Publications Association, Ltd., for his skillful efforts in making these two books one. It is our hope that serious students of the Word will find fresh insight into the meaning of our sharing the life of our risen Lord.

The Publisher

Where to Start These Studies

1 Corinthians 2:11-15

FIRST MAN   SECOND MAN

1 Corinthians 15:45-50

Adam   Christ

Living Soul, v. 45   Quickening Spirit, v. 45
Natural, v. 46   Spiritual, v. 46
Earthly, v. 47   Heavenly, v. 47

NEW MAN
Saint

Earthly and Heavenly Image, v. 48
Earthly Effaced by Heavenly Image, v. 49
Divinely Inherited Kingdom of God, v. 50

Christian psychology is based on the knowledge of the Lord Jesus Christ, not on the knowledge of ourselves. It is not the study of human nature analyzed and expounded, but the study of the new life that is born in us through the redemption of our Lord. And the only standard of that new life is our Lord Himself; He is formed in us by regeneration (see Galatians 1:15-16). We are apt to start with the way we are made naturally and to transfer our reasonings on that to Jesus Christ, inferring that to understand ourselves is to understand Him. In Christian psychology we have not to introspect as we do in natural psychology; we have to accept the revelations given to us in and through our Lord Jesus Christ; that is, we must take all our bearings from the Son of God, not from our natural wits. We have not to study and understand ourselves, but to understand the manifestation in us of the life of the Son of God who became Son of Man, the Lord Jesus Christ.

According to the Bible, there are only two men: Adam and Jesus Christ. God deals with them as the representatives of the human race, not as individuals. All the members of the human race are grouped around these two men. The first Adam is called "the son of God"; the last Adam is *the* Son of God, and we are made sons of God by the last Adam. The Christian is neither Adam nor Jesus Christ: The Christian is a new man in Christ Jesus. The first Adam and the last Adam are the only two men according to God's norm, and they both came into this world direct from the hand of God.

First Man

Living Soul. "The first man Adam became a living being" (1 Corinthians 15:45). Beware of dividing man up into body, soul, and spirit. Man *is* body, soul, and spirit. Soul is the expression of man's personal spirit in his body. Spirit means I, myself, the incalculable being that is "me," the essence that expresses itself in the soul. The immortal part of a man is not his soul, but his spirit. Man's spirit is as indestructible as almighty God; the expression of his spirit in the soul depends on the body. In the Bible, the soul is always referred to in connection with the body. The soul is the holder of the body and spirit together, and when the body disappears, the soul disappears, but the essential personality of the man remains. In the resurrection, there is another body and instantly the soul life is manifested again (see John 5:28-29). It is not a resurrection of spirit; that is,. personality that never dies, but of body and soul.

A "living being" means man expressing himself as God designed he should. God created man a splendid moral being, fitted to rule the earth and air and sea, but he was not to rule himself; God was to be his master, and man was to turn his natural life into a spiritual life by obedience. Had Adam done so, the members of the human race would have gone on developing until they were transfigured in the presence of God; there would have been no death. Death to us has become natural, but the Bible reveals it to be abnormal. Adam refused to turn the natural into the spiritual; he took dominion over himself and thereby became the introducer of the heredity of sin into the human race (see Romans 5:12) and instantly lost his control over the earth and air and sea. The entrance of sin means that the connection with God has gone and the disposition of self-realization, my right to myself, has come in its place.

"For by Him all things were created . . ." (Colossians 1:16). Did God then create sin? Sin is not a creation; sin is the outcome of a relationship that God never ordained, a relationship set up between the man God created and the being God created who became the devil. God did not create sin, but He holds Himself responsible for the possibility of sin, and the proof that He does so is in the cross of our Lord Jesus Christ. Calvary is God's responsibility undertaken and carried through as redemption. The essential nature of sin is my claim to my right to myself, and when sin entered in, the connection between man and God was instantly severed; at-one-ness was no longer possible.

Natural. "However, the spiritual is not first, but the natural, and afterward the spiritual" (v. 46). Unless we are born again, we will always be "natural" men. In John 3, our Lord is not talking about sin and hell; He is talking to a religious leader, a clean-living, upright, good, noble man—a natural man—and it was to him that He said, "Do not marvel that I said to you, 'You must be born again.' " The general idea is that a man must be a scoundrel before Jesus Christ can do anything for him. The average preaching of the gospel deals mainly with the scenic cases, with people who have gone through exceptional experiences. None of the early disciples had had these exceptional experiences; they saw in Jesus Christ what they had never seen before—a man from another realm—and they began to long after what He stood for. We preach to men as if they were conscious of being dying sinners; they are not, they are having a good time, and our talk about being born again is from a domain of which they know nothing. The natural man does not want to be born again.

Earthly. "The first man was of the earth, made of dust" (v. 47). This is man's glory, not his shame, because it is in a creature made of the earth that God is going to manifest His glory. We are apt to think that being made of the earth is our humiliation, but it is the very point that is made much of in God's Word. In the Middle Ages, it was taught that sin resided in the actual fleshly body and therefore the body was a clog and a hindrance. The Bible says that the body is the temple of the Holy Spirit, not a thing to be despised. Sin is not in having a body and a nature that needs to be sacrificed; sin is in refusing to sacrifice them at the call of God. Sin is a disposition that rules the body, and regeneration means not only that we need not obey the disposition of sin, but that we can be absolutely delivered from it (see Romans 6:6).

Second Man

Quickening Spirit. "The last Adam became a life-giving spirit" (v. 45). Jesus Christ came into the human race from the outside, and when we are born again, His life comes into us from the outside. Jesus Christ is the normal man, and in His relationship to God, to the devil, to sin, and to man we see the expression in human nature of what He calls "eternal life." We try to enter the life of Jesus in the wrong way. We do not enter into His life by imitation; we enter into it by its entering into us by means of His death. Jesus Christ gives us His life—His Holy Spirit. When we ask God for the Holy Spirit, we receive the very nature of God—Holy Spirit. We become regenerate, born from above, by the gift of life from the last Adam. Then we have to live in obedience to the Spirit that has come into our spirit.

The records in the Gospels are given, not so much that we might understand the person of our Lord from the natural standpoint, but that we might understand how to exhibit His life in us when we are born from above. We have to take our instructions for this from Jesus Christ. The danger is that we will praise God's salvation and sovereign grace while we refuse to manifest His salvation in our human nature.

Spiritual. "However, the spiritual is not first, but the natural, and afterward the spiritual" (v. 46). That which is not earthly, but in accordance with the nature of spirit. There are counterfeit spiritualities, but the spirituality of Jesus Christ is a holy spirituality. Jesus Christ worked from a spiritual standpoint, the Spirit of God so indwelt Him that His spirituality was manifested in His ordinary soul life.

Heavenly. ". . . the second Man is the Lord from heaven" (v. 47). The second Man is the Son of God historically manifested and the prophecy of what the human race is going to be. In Him we deal with God as man, the God-man, the representative of the whole human race in one person. Jesus Christ is not a being with two personalities; He is Son of God (the exact expression of almighty God) and Son of Man (the presentation of God's normal man). As Son of God, He reveals what God is like (see John 14:9); as Son of Man, He mirrors what the human race will be like on the basis of redemption—a perfect oneness between God and man (see Ephesians 4:13).

New Man

Earthly and Heavenly Image. "As was the man of dust, so also are those who are made of dust; and as is the heavenly man, so also are those also who are heavenly" (v. 48). The "natural" has not life in itself; therefore, we must be born from above. To be born from above means that we are lifted into heavenly places in our personal spirit by the Holy Spirit who comes into us. He quickens us throughout. The Holy Spirit does in us what Jesus Christ did for us. The Holy Spirit is essential deity, and He energizes our spirit and presences us with deity as our Lord was presenced. Holy Spirit never becomes our spirit; He quickens our spirit, and instantly we begin to express a new soul.

When God's Spirit comes into our personality, our soul life begins to be upset, and the bodily life often gets disorganized. Health is simply the balance of our bodily life with external circumstances. Anything that upsets the equilibrium on the inside upsets the bodily equilibrium on the outside; consequently, when a man is convicted of sin, his "beauty melts away like a moth" (Psalm 39:11). Beauty means the perfectly ordered completeness of a man's nature. A man into whom the Spirit of God has entered is for a while out of harmony. The Spirit of God brings upset and conviction: He throws light on what is dark, He searches the recesses of the disposition; consequently, the preaching of the gospel, while it awakens an intense craving, awakens an equally intense resentment. Conviction of sin means that we realize that our natural life is based on a disposition that will not have Jesus Christ. If the man will obey the Holy Spirit, the new balance of holiness will be set up—the balance of his disposition with the law of God. Then he must obey God's will in his body, and this will mean crucifying the flesh with its affections and lusts (see Galatians 5:24).

Earthly Effaced by Heavenly Image. "And as we have borne the image of the man of dust, we shall also bear the image of the heavenly Man" (v. 49). Have you never seen the earthly effaced by the heavenly? Watch the face of a man or woman who has been born again and who is going on with God. There is a change in the features that cannot be defined. The explanation of it is that when God makes us all over again, our bodies are molded by the new Spirit within and begin to manifest that Spirit (see 2 Corinthians 5:17). When we receive the Holy Spirit, He lifts us into the realm where Jesus Christ lives, and all things become new. We cannot estimate Jesus Christ along the natural line. He does not belong to this order of things, and He says that if we want to belong to His order, we must be born from above (see John 3:3, 5). Tolstoy taught the principles of Jesus, but he ignored the need to be born again. Let a man receive the Holy Spirit, and Jesus Christ will do in him all that he ever imagined He would do, and he will find that it works all the time.

Divinely Inherited Kingdom of God. "Now this I say, brethren, that flesh and blood cannot inherit the kingdom of God; nor does corruption inherit incorruption" (v. 50). The characteristics of the natural man, apart from sin, are independence and individuality. Individuality is the strong and emphatic and somewhat ugly husk that guards the personal life. Individuality is a right characteristic in a child, but in a man or woman it is not only objectionable but dangerous, because it means independence of God as well as of other people, and independence of God is of the very nature of sin. The only way we can get rid of the pride of individuality and become one with Jesus Christ is by being born from above.

Sin dwells in human nature, but the Bible makes it very clear that it is an abnormal thing, that it has no right there, and that it does not belong to human nature as God designed it. Sin has come into human nature and perverted and twisted it. The redemption of God through our Lord Jesus Christ delivers human nature from sin, and then begins the possibility of the manifestation of the life of Jesus in our mortal flesh. We are saved by God's grace, but, thank God, we have something to do. We must take care to meet God's supernatural work of grace by our human obedience. When we have been delivered from sin, the characteristics of our natural life have to be sacrificed, not murdered, not denied in the sense of being ignored, but sacrificed; that is, transformed into agreement with the heavenly by obedience (see Ephesians 5:23). We are saved from sin and readjusted to God, but we are still human beings, and we have to take the trouble to actually prove what God has really done in us.

God never saves men and women the trouble of manifesting the fact that He has made them His sons and daughters. We begin all right, but it is easy to get switched off. If we do not continue to live in the right place, we will get back into "Adam" sympathies. It is on "Adam" sympathies that much of our Christian work is based, not on sympathy with Jesus Christ, the last Adam. Satan's temptations of our Lord were based on sympathy with the first Adam: "Put man's needs first." Jesus Christ says, "Do not think first of the needs of the people: think first of the commands of God" (Mark 12:29-31).

Natural individuality holds strongly to natural relationships. The natural relationships on which individuality is based are these: father, mother, brothers and sisters, husband and wife, children, self-interest. These are the relationships with which our Lord says we are likely to clash if we are going to be His disciples. If the clash comes, He says it must be instant obedience to Him (see Luke 14:26). Our obedience to Jesus Christ is going to cost other people a great deal. And if we refuse to go on because of the cost to them or because of the stab and the jeer, we may find that we have prevented the call of God coming to other lives; whereas if we will go through with God, all these natural relationships will be given to our credit spiritually at the last.

Beginning

Some Things to Remember

The Revelation of Christ (Matthew 16:16-17)
The Records of Christ (John 5:39)
The Realization of Christ (1 Corinthians 1:30)

Some Things to Realize

The Evangelical Experience (The Synoptic Gospels and John)
The Examined Experience (The Epistles)
The Exercised Experience (The Present Obedience)

It is easy to put up our Lord as an example, but according to the New Testament, He is much more. He is the Redeemer, one who can reproduce His own life in us. To be born from above means more than conversion. It means that Christ is formed in us, and the Christ in us must be exactly like the Christ outside us. The characteristics that Jesus Christ exhibited in His human life are to be exhibited in the Christian. Christian psychology is based on our realization of who the Lord Jesus Christ is and on an understanding of His life in us.

There is a difference between sight and the organ of sight. Most of us are quite content to see; we do not bother about the organ of sight. But when something goes wrong with the organ of sight, those of us who can see only are of no use to put the eye right. Then we must consult someone who knows how the organ of sight is constructed. The Christian worker is apt to say, "Oh well, I have been saved by God's grace, and that is sufficient." It may be sufficient for you, but if you are going to be "a workman who does not need to be ashamed," you must do more than be saved, you must take the trouble to find out what the Bible says about that salvation. Most of us are like the folks who are content with being able to see. But the organ of sight spiritually in many has gone wrong, and we have no knowledge of how to deal with it. All we can do is give our testimony. That is not good enough. The point of this study is not only that we might understand salvation for ourselves, but that we might understand how to assist others.

Some Things to Remember

The Revelation of Christ. "And Simon Peter answered and said, 'You are the Christ, the Son of the living God.' Jesus answered and said to him, 'Blessed are you, Simon Bar-Jona, for flesh and blood has not revealed this to you, but My Father who is in heaven" (Matthew 16:16-17). The Lord Jesus Christ is not a commonsensical fact; that is, we do not understand Him by means of our common sense. The disciples at this stage only knew Jesus Christ by means of their common sense—by their eyes and ears and all the powers of common sense men—they had never discerned who He was. Our Lord is a revelation fact, and when Peter confessed, "You are the Christ, the Son of the living God," Jesus Christ recognized from whom he had received the revelation—not from his common sense, but from God. Is Jesus Christ a revelation to me, or is He simply a historical character?

The Bible is the universe of revelation facts; the natural world is the universe of common sense facts. Our means of communication with the two universes is totally different. We come in contact with the natural universe by our senses; our intellect has to be curious. Scientific knowledge, which is systematized common sense, is based on intense intellectual curiosity. Curiosity in the natural world is right, not wrong, and if we are not intellectually curious, we shall never know anything. God never encourages laziness.

When we come to the universe of the Bible, the revelation facts about God, intellectual curiosity is not of the slightest use. Our senses are no good here; we cannot find out God by searching. We may have inferences from our commonsensical thinking that we call God, but these are mere abstractions. We can only get at the facts that are revealed in the Bible by faith. Faith is not credulity; faith is my personal spirit obeying God. The Bible does not deal in commonsensical facts; the natural universe deals in commonsensical facts, and we get at these by our senses. The Bible deals with revelation facts—facts we cannot get at by our common sense, facts we may be pleased to make light of by our common sense. For instance, Jesus Christ is a revelation fact; sin is another; the devil is another; the Holy Spirit is another. Not one of these is a commonsensical fact. If a man were merely a commonsensical individual, he could do very well without God.

To get scientific knowledge we must use our common sense, but if we are going to know the facts with which Jesus Christ deals, the facts that He says belong to the kingdom of God, we must have them revealed to us. "Do not marvel that I say to you, You must be born again before you can come into contact with the domain in which I live." The domain in which Jesus Christ lives is the domain of Bible facts. How are we to get the revelation of Jesus Christ? Very simply, if we want it. Jesus Christ said that the Holy Spirit would glorify Him, and we can receive the Holy Spirit for the asking (see Luke 11:13), the meaning of which cannot be gotten at by common sense. Have we ever received the Holy Spirit? If we refuse any one way of getting at the truth because we do not like that way, we are dishonest.

The Records of Christ. "You search the Scriptures, for in them you think you have eternal life . . ." (John 5:39). The Scriptures, from Genesis to Revelation, are all revelations of Jesus Christ. The context of the Bible is our Lord Himself, and until we get rightly related to Him, the Bible is no more to us than an ordinary book. Common sense does not reveal Jesus Christ; to common sense He is nothing more than a Nazarene carpenter who lived twenty centuries ago. No natural man can know Jesus Christ (see Matthew 11:27). Higher criticism, so called, works on the lines of common sense; consequently, when it deals with our Lord (whose highest sense is not common sense, but deity), He has to be explained away—His Person is "dissolved by analysis" (see 1 John 4:1-3). The findings of higher criticism may be logically proved, but the biggest facts in life are not logical. If they were, we should be able to calculate our ends and make sure of things on rational logical lines. Logical truth is merely the explanation of facts that common sense has gathered. Men say, "I must have these things proved to my reason." How much good spiritually did a man ever get by proving things to his reason?

In spiritual matters, logical processes do not count. Curiosity does not count, nor argument, nor reasoning: These are of no avail for spiritual discernment. There is only one golden rule for spiritual discernment and that is obedience. We learn more by five minutes' obedience than by ten years' study. Logic and reasoning are methods of expounding reality, but we do not get at reality by our intellect. Reality is only gotten at by our conscience. When we deal with the records of Christ, we are dealing with fundamental realities. And there is nothing logical about faith; it is of the nature of life.

After we are born again, the Bible becomes a new book to us, and we search the Scriptures, not to get "life" out of them, but to know more about Jesus Christ. "You search the Scriptures, for in them you think you have eternal life, . . . but you are not willing to come to Me that you may have life" (John 5:39-40). The vital relationship that the Christian has to the Bible is not that he worships the letter, but that the Holy Spirit makes the words of the Bible spirit and life to him. Before we are born from above, the Bible is only an ordinary book; after we are born from above, the Bible becomes a universe of revelation facts whereby we feed our knowledge of Jesus Christ.

The Realization of Christ. "But of Him you are in Christ Jesus, who became for us wisdom from God—and righteousness and sanctification and redemption" (1 Corinthians 1:30). In Proverbs 8, we read of preincarnate wisdom, and in John's gospel that wisdom is referred to as the logos, or word. Historically, the Word was called Jesus Christ. The whole wisdom of God has come down to the shores of our lives in a flesh and blood man, and John says, we have seen Him and we know Him. How are we to realize Jesus Christ? He says "Come to Me," and there is no profounder word in human language than that. The one thing that keeps us from coming to Jesus Christ is obstinacy; we will do anything rather than come. It is not God's will that a man should be smashed before he is saved. It is the man's obstinacy that does it. There is no need to go through the agonies and distresses that so many do go through, it is because we will not come. If we want to realize Jesus Christ, He says "Come to Me," and when we do come, God makes Him "for us wisdom from God—and righteousness and sanctification and redemption." If Jesus Christ is not revealed to us, it is because we have views of our own, and we want to bend everything to those views. To realize Christ we must come to Him. That is, we must learn to trust someone other than ourselves, and to do this, we must deliberately efface ourselves.

Devotion and piety are apt to be the greatest opponents of Jesus Christ, because we devote ourselves to devotion instead of to Him. To surrender to God is not to surrender to the fact that we have surrendered. That is not coming at all. To come means that we come to God in complete abandonment and give ourselves right over to Him and leave ourselves in His hands. The Lord Jesus Christ is the one person to whom we ought to yield, and we must be perfectly certain that it is to Himself that we are yielding. Do not be sorry if other appeals find you stiff-necked and unyielding; but be sorry if, when He says "Come to Me," you do not come. The attitude of coming is that the will resolutely lets go of everything and deliberately commits all to Him.

Some Things to Realize

The Evangelical Experience. The Synoptics are the first three gospels; John's writings include his epistles and the Apocalypse as well as his gospel. Our Lord never talked of conversion and regeneration and sanctification in stages, neither does the apostle John. If we get hold of books that talk in the stages of experience and then come to the gospels where those stages are not marked, we are apt to get embarrassed. The gospels always present truth in "nugget" form, and if we want to know the stages of evangelical experience, we must go to the epistles, which beat out into negotiable gold the nuggets of truth presented by our Lord. In John 3, our Lord is not talking about the stages of conversion; He is talking in the great terms of what He came to do—to make redemption the basis of human life. We can introduce other things into His words if we like, but we must not say He said them. Our Lord is not examining the evangelical experience, He is stating it. He said to Nicodemus, "You must be born again." That is not a command, but the statement of a foundation fact.

We mean by the evangelical experience an experience based on the fact that the cross of our Lord Jesus Christ, that is, His death, is the gateway for us into His life. We delight to hear about the life of Jesus. It captivates our imagination to hear sermons on following in His steps until we find that we cannot begin to do it. "Jesus Christ was a great teacher." So He was, an amazing teacher, but where are you going to begin to carry out what He says? The Sermon on the Mount is exquisitely beautiful teaching, and it fascinates us so long as we deal with it intellectually only, but when it comes down to our daily life, practical and sordid and real, we find we cannot begin to carry it out. We may give our mental assent to it, but our actual life won't walk that road. The teachings of Jesus must produce despair, because if He meant what He said, where are we in regard to it? The revelation of the New Testament is not that Jesus Christ came to teach primarily but that He came to redeem, to make us what He teaches we should be. Then the teachings of Jesus become the description of what God has undertaken to make a man if he will let the power of God work through him. Redemption means that Jesus Christ can give us His own disposition, and all the standards He gives are based on that disposition; that is, His teaching is for the life He puts in us. We enter into the life of Jesus by means of His death; that is our only door of entrance.

We may try to batter through some other way if we choose—through Bethlehem, through the teachings of Jesus, but we cannot get in. Those ways produce frauds and humbugs. If a teacher or preacher has not an evangelical experience himself, his preaching and teaching will degenerate into mere intellectual common sense. It may be smeared over with the teachings of Jesus and may sound beautiful, but there is no power in it to alter anything in us. We cannot get into the life of Jesus by imitation, by trying to do the right thing, because something in us will not do it. We can only enter in by identification with His death. The cross of Jesus Christ is not the cross of a martyr, but the door whereby God keeps open house for the universe. Anyone can go in through that door. The cross is the historical presentation of the one reality there is—redemption. And if we come to Jesus, that reality works in us by the incoming of the Holy Spirit, and we find that we are brought into a new kingdom. There is something totally different now; we can show in our bodily life the disposition of Jesus Christ, which we receive by means of His cross; we can begin now to live the kind of life He lived.

The Examined Experience. The evangelical experience is stated in the synoptics and in John's writings in its great wonderful revelation form, not in its examined stages; but if we want to have the experience examined and stated so that we can see its stages and get a grasp of it, we must turn to the epistles. The epistles are the posthumous writings of the ascended Lord; He sent the Holy Spirit, and the "pens" used were the apostles, and the expositions given are from the Holy Spirit. Our Lord's teachings and the expositions given in the epistles stand or fall together. The epistles are our guide in finding out the stages of the experience. There we will find all about conversion, about regeneration, and about sanctification. We will find the stages all carefully set forth, but we must take the trouble to find them out. Acts 26:18 gives the examined experience in condensed form better than any other passage in the New Testament. We so often try to worry out Jesus Christ's statements apart from the guidance of the Holy Spirit. It is the workman of God who can rightly divide the word of truth, who becomes the expert in the things of God, and when anyone is being led astray by false doctrines, the expert can show what is wrong.

The Exercised Experience. If we have experienced regeneration, we must not only talk about the experience, we must exercise it and work out what God has worked in (see Philippians 2:12-13). We have to show it in our fingertips, in our tongue, and in our bodily contact with other people, and as we obey God, we find we have a wealth of power on the inside. The question of forming habits on the basis of the grace of God is a very vital one. To ignore it is to fall into the snare of the Pharisee: the grace of God is praised; Jesus Christ is praised; the redemption is praised, but the practical everyday life evades working it out. If we refuse to practice, it is not God's grace that fails when a crisis comes, but our own nature. When the crisis comes, we ask God to help us, but He cannot if we have not made our nature an ally. The practicing is ours, not God's. God regenerates us and puts us in contact with all His divine resources, but He cannot make us walk according to His will. If we will obey the Spirit of God and practice through our physical life all that God has put in our hearts by His Spirit, then when the crisis comes, we shall find that we have not only God's grace to stand by us but our own nature also. The crisis is passed without any disaster, and the soul is built up into a stronger attitude toward God.

His Birth and Our New Birth

His Birth in History (Luke 1:35)
The Highest. The Holiest. The Lowliest.

His Birth in Me (Galatians 4:19)
The Lowliest. The Holiest. The Highest.
Do I come to Jesus because of what they say, or
because of what I see? (John 1:12-13)
Do I seek for signs of the kingdom of God, or do I see
the rule of God? (John 3:3)
Do I seek to stop sinning, or have I stopped sinning?
(1 John 3:9)

If we study the characteristics of the Christian soul, we
must not look to Adam or to our own experience, but to
Jesus Christ, who is our foundation. Christian psychology is
the study of a supernatural life made natural in our human
life by the redemption. We do not know Jesus Christ by
knowing ourselves; to think we do is a modern fallacy.
". . . No one knows the Son except the Father. Nor does
anyone know the Father except the Son, and he to whom
the Son wills to reveal Him" (Matthew 11:27). If we are
ever going to know the Father and the Son, we must have
their nature, and we are not born with it. The meaning of
new birth is that we know God by a vital relationship, not
only by our intellect. "As many as received Him, to them He
gave the right to become children of God . . . who were

born, not of blood, nor of the will of the flesh, nor of the will of man, but of God" (John 1:12-13). The characteristics of the new-birth life are not the characteristics of our Lord's life, which we have to see manifested in our natural life. Jesus Christ sets the standard of God's life in us. We have not to ask what good men have experienced, but to go direct to the Lord Jesus Christ and study His exhibition of the character of God's normal man.

His Birth in History. "And the angel answered and said to her, 'The Holy Spirit shall come upon you, and the power of the Highest will overshadow you; therefore, also, that Holy One who is to be born will be called the Son of God'" (Luke 1:35).

Jesus Christ was born into this world, not from it. He came into history from the outside of history; He did not evolve out of history. Our Lord's birth was an advent: He did not come from the human race, He came into it from above. Jesus Christ is not the best human being, He is a being who cannot be accounted for by the human race at all. He is God incarnate, not man becoming God, but God coming into human flesh, coming into it from the outside. His life is the highest and the holiest entering in at the lowliest door. Our Lord entered history by the virgin Mary.

His Birth in Me. "My little children, for whom I labor in birth again until Christ is formed in you" (Galatians 4:19).

Just as our Lord came into human history from the outside, so He must come into us from the outside. Have we allowed our personal human lives to become a "Bethlehem" for the Son of God? The modern tendency is to talk of birth from beneath, not of birth from above; of something rising up out of our unconscious life into our conscious life, not of something coming into us from above. This preaching has so permeated people's views today that many who name the name of Christ and are supposed to be preaching His gospel are at the same time undermining the very foundations of their own faith.

We cannot enter into the realm of the kingdom of God unless we are born from above by a birth totally unlike natural birth (see John 3:5). People have the idea that because there is good in human nature (and thank God, there is a lot of good in human nature), that therefore the Spirit of God is in every man naturally, meaning that the Spirit of God in us will become the Christ in us if we let Him have His way. Take that view if you like, but never say it is the view of the New Testament. It certainly is not the Lord's view. He said to Nicodemus, "Do not marvel that I said to you, 'You must be born again' "; that is, something must come into you from the outside. Today, people are dethroning Jesus Christ and belittling the need of salvation by making new birth to mean nothing more than a rising up from beneath. The conception of new birth in the New Testament is of something that enters into us, not of something that springs out of us.

We are dealing with new birth as our Lord presents it. The Holy Spirit, sent by Jesus after He was glorified, is the One who expounds the various stages in the experience of new birth. Our Lord never speaks in stages of experience, and the reason people divide into stages what our Lord said to Nicodemus is that they have taken their light from the epistles. We are not dealing just now with the stages of experience, but with the fact of new birth—Christ formed in me. This does not correspond to what is evangelically known as being saved, but rather to the Methodist doctrine of entire sanctification, which is but the beginning of the purpose of the Christian life. If we are to understand how the new birth is to work, we must look at the epistles. Paul alludes to the new-birth life at work when he says, "I labor in birth again until Christ is formed in you." It is the travailing of one who has himself been born from above. How many of us know anything about this travailing for those who have been really quickened by the Holy Spirit until Christ is formed in them? We are apt to rejoice in the number of souls who are evangelically described as being saved, but what becomes of them all? They have been introduced into the kingdom of God, but as yet there is no evidence that Christ is formed in them. Jesus Christ sent His disciples to "disciple" all nations. The regeneration of souls is God's work; our work as saved souls is to work under His orders on the basis of redemption, and Galatians 4:19 is an indication of what that work is. "Therefore pray the Lord of the harvest, to send out laborers into His harvest" (Matthew 9:38). The labor is prayer. We labor on the ground of our Lord's redemption in simple confidence in Him.

Do I come to Jesus because of what they say, or because of what I see? "But as many as received Him, to them He gave the right to become children of God . . . who were born, not of blood, nor of the will of the flesh, nor of the will of man, but of God (John 1:12-13). The life after new birth has very simple characteristics. To know whether we have been born from above, we must be guided by the revelation given by our Lord. One great characteristic of new birth is that we come to Jesus not only because of what we have heard about Him, but because of what we see He is to us now. Our Lord did not send forth His disciples on the ground of what He had done for them; He sent them because they had seen Him after His resurrection and because they knew who He was, "Now go and tell My brethren." Mary Magdalene was His first apostle, she was the one out of whom our Lord had cast seven demons, but that was not to be the ground of her going. It was not until she had realized who her Lord was after His resurrection and the altered relationship in which she now stood to Him, that He said, "Go." If Christ is formed in us, the great characteristic is that we know Him and perceive Him for ourselves. We do not need anyone to tell us about Him now. He is our Lord and Master.

Another characteristic of new birth is that Jesus Christ is easily first. Where do we go in a crisis? If we are born from above and Jesus Christ is Lord and Master, we will go direct as a homing pigeon to Him. The reason the majority of us know so little about the lordship of Jesus Christ is that we only know the quickening of His Spirit; we have not gone on to the experience of Christ being formed in us. We know a great deal about the evangelical doctrine of being saved from hell but very little about Galatians 1:15-16. In Acts 1:8, our Lord said this striking thing: ". . . You shall be witnesses to Me . . . ." When Christ is formed in us, we are a satisfaction to our Lord and Master wherever He places us. The point of importance is to know that we are just exactly where He has engineered our circumstances. There is no "foreign field" to our Lord. The reason we feel called to foreign mission work is because God introduces His own nature into us when we are identified with Jesus Christ (see John 3:16). We know what the nature of God is like because we see it manifested in Jesus Christ. As soon as Christ is formed in us, His nature begins to work through our hearts and to alter our conceptions.

Do I seek for signs of the kingdom of God, or do I see the rule of God? "Jesus answered and said to him, 'Most assuredly, I say to you, unless one is born again, he cannot see the kingdom of God" (John 3:3). Another evidence of new birth is that we see the rule of God. We no longer see the haphazard of chance or fate, but by the experience of new birth we are enabled to see the rule of God everywhere. "Who has believed our report? And to whom has the arm of the Lord been revealed?" (Isaiah 53:1), literally, "Who has the power to discern the arm of the Lord?" We all see the common occurrences of our daily life, but who among us can perceive the arm of the Lord behind them? The saint recognizes in all the ordinary circumstances of his life the hand of God and the rule of God, and Jesus says we cannot do that unless we are born from above. In the beginning we only discern the rule of God in exceptional things, in crises like a friendship, or marriage, or death, but that is an elementary stage. As we go on, we learn to see God's rule in all the ordinary haphazard circumstances of a common sense life, and to say, "I shall never think of anything my heavenly Father will forget. Then why should I worry?" Are we irritable and worried? Then do not let us say we are born from above, because if what Jesus says is true, how can we worry? Worry means one of two things: private sin or the absence of new birth. Nothing happens by chance to a saint, no matter how haphazard it seems. It is the order of God, and the experience of new birth means that we are able to discern the order of God.

The Sermon on the Mount is not a set of principles to be obeyed apart from identification with Jesus Christ. The Sermon on the Mount is a statement of the life we will live when the Holy Spirit is getting His way with us. The Holy Spirit applies the principle of Jesus to our circumstances as God engineers them, and we have to see that we exhibit the new-birth life at work. Tolstoy made the blunder of applying the principles of Jesus straight away to practical circumstances while he ignored the need for the new birth. Jesus Christ does not lay down the statements in the Sermon on the Mount as principles and say, "Now work them out," He is describing what the new life is in its working from His standpoint. When circumstances arise by God's providential engineering, and the Holy Spirit brings back some word to our remembrance, are we going to obey our Lord in that particular? Never debate when the Holy Spirit brings back a word of Jesus Christ. A fanatic is one who takes the statements of Jesus and tries to live up to the standard of them while he ignores the necessity of personal relationship with God through new birth. We have not to live according to maxim, but according to the new life in us in which Jesus Christ is manifested.

Do I seek to stop sinning, or have I stopped sinning? "Whoever is born of God does not sin; for His seed remains in him; and he cannot sin, because he has been born of God" (1 John 3:9). Do we seek to stop sinning, or have we stopped sinning? We are always inclined to make theoretical what God makes practical. Learned divines and others talk about the sin question and make it a doctrinal matter of dispute. In the Bible it is never: Should a Christian sin? The Bible puts it emphatically: A Christian must not sin. The confusion arises when the practical experimental doctrine is made a philosophical doctrine to do with God's election. Deliverance from sin is not a question of God's election, but of an experience in human life that God demands. The effective working of the new-birth life in us is that we do not commit sin, not merely that we have the power not to sin, but that we have stopped sinning—a much more practical thing.

The one thing that will enable us to stop sinning is the experience of new birth; that is, entire sanctification. When we are born into the new realm, the life of God is born in us, and the life of God in us cannot sin (1 John 3:9) . That does not mean that we cannot sin; it means that if we obey the life of God in us, we need not sin. God never takes away our power to disobey; if He did, our obedience would be of no value, for we should cease to be morally responsible. By regeneration God puts in us the power not to sin. Our human nature is just the same after new birth as before, but the mainspring is different. Before new birth we sin because we cannot help it; after new birth we need not sin. There is a difference between sin and sins: Sin is a disposition and is never spoken of as being forgiven, a disposition must be cleansed; sins are acts for which we are responsible. Sin is a thing we are born with, and we cannot touch it; God touches sin in redemption. If we have been trying to be holy, it is a sure sign we are not. Christians are born, not made. They are not produced by imitation, nor by praying and vowing; they are produced by new birth (see John 3:7). "By the grace of God I am what I am."

The characteristic of new birth is that we deliberately obey all that God reveals through His Spirit. We yield ourselves so completely to God that Christ is formed in us. When He is formed in us, the characteristics of His life in our mortal flesh are that we see Jesus for ourselves; we see the rule of God; and we quit sinning—all by the wonder of His supernatural new birth in us. And that is how it works throughout.

His Humanity and Incarnation

The only "Life" of the Lord Jesus is the New Testament.
There are phases of the life of our Lord presented in the
New Testament that no other life, so-called, deals with. If
you start with the theory that Jesus Christ was a man who
became God, you have to leave out any number of New
Testament facts. If you say that Jesus Christ was God and
His manhood a seeming phase, you have to leave out other
facts. The Person of Jesus Christ revealed in the New
Testament is unique—the God-Man, the representative of
the whole human race in one Person. Jesus Christ is not a
being with two personalities; He is the Son of God, the
exact expression of almighty God, and Son of Man—the
presentation of God's normal Man.

A great many of the books written on what is called "the
psychology of Jesus" are an attempt to understand the Person
of Jesus through an understanding of ourselves. That is fatally
misleading because Jesus Christ does not begin where we
begin. "All things have been delivered to me by my Father: and
no one knows the Son, except the Father . . ." (Matthew
11:27). The basis of the Person of Jesus is not the basis of ours
unless we have been born again of the Holy Spirit. The
tendency today to "annul"—that is, "dissolve by analysis"—
the Person of Jesus, does untold damage to moral and spiritual
understanding (see 1 John 4:1-3). As soon as we introduce a
rationalism that does not accept the New Testament
revelation, we get confused. We will not bring to the subject

the innocence of mind that the Spirit of God demands; we bring objections that spring from preconceived notions.

Analogy of the First Adam and Last Adam (Romans 5:12, 19)

There are only two Men in the Bible: Adam and Jesus Christ, "with all humanity hanging at their girdles."

And the LORD God formed man of the dust of the ground, and breathed into his nostrils the breath of life; and man became a living soul. (Genesis 2:7)

The Holy Spirit will come upon you, and the power of the Highest will overshadow you; therefore, also, that Holy One who is to be born will be called the Son of God. (Luke 1:35)

The New Testament reveals that the birth of Jesus was an Advent, not a beginning—an Advent that put Him on the plane, humanly speaking, that Adam was on. The first Adam and the last Adam came direct from the hand of God.

God did not create Adam holy; He created him innocent, without self-consciousness (as we understand the word) before God. The one thing Adam was conscious of was God, and only of himself in relation to the Being whose commands he was to fulfill. The main trend of his spirit was toward God.

Adam was intended by God to take part in his own development by a series of moral choices whereby he would transform innocence into holiness. Adam failed to do this. Jesus Christ came on the same platform as Adam and did not fail. Supposing Adam had transformed the natural life into the spiritual by obedience. What would have happened?

Transfiguration. He would have "spiritualized" the natural life and made it all that God wanted it to be. The natural life is neither good nor bad, moral nor immoral; it is the principle within that makes it good or bad, moral or immoral.

"And the Child grew and became strong in spirit, filled with wisdom; and the grace of God was upon Him" (Luke 2:40). The innocence of Jesus was not the innocence of a baby born into our order of things; it was the innocence of Adam as God created him, the innocence of an untried possibility of holiness. Innocence is never safe, it is simply full of possibility. The holiness of God is absolute, not progressive; that is, it knows no development by antagonism. Man's holiness must be progressive. The holiness of Jesus developed through antagonism because He revealed what a holy man should be.

Our Lord transformed innocence into holiness by a series of moral choices. Satan tempted Him along this line: "Do God's will according to Your own understanding; don't sacrifice the life of nature to the will of God." Jesus invariably made one answer: "For I have come down from heaven, not to do my own will, but the will of Him who sent Me" (John 6:38).

How are we to "follow His steps"? By imitating Jesus? We cannot begin to do that. How are we going to have the innocence that Jesus had? In one way only: by being born from above. "Do not marvel that I said to you, 'You must be born again'" (John 3:7). We can be brought into a state of pristine, childlike innocence before God by the regenerating work of His grace. God does something infinitely grander than give a man a new start: He remakes him from the inside. We have the power, because we have received it, to transform the natural into the spiritual even as Jesus did, because the life generated into us is His own life.

Resources of Life. God created Adam to "have dominion over the fish of the sea, over the birds of the air, and over every living thing that moves on the earth" (Genesis 1:28). The one thing Adam was not to have dominion over was himself. God was to have dominion over him, and Adam had to partake in his own development by obeying God's rule over him, not his own wisdom. The source of life in Adam was his obedience to God.

Jesus Christ, the last Adam, states over and over again, ". . . the Son can do nothing of Himself" (John 5:19, 30; see also John 7:16, 49; 8:28; 14:10).

The birth of Jesus throws a striking light on our regeneration. Our new birth is the birth of the Son of God into our human nature, and our human nature has to be transfigured by the indwelling life of the Son of God. We have the power now to sacrifice the life of nature to the will of God, keeping our minds dependent on Jesus Christ as He was dependent on God. Today the characteristic is spiritual insubordination; we will not bring "every thought into captivity to the obedience of Christ."

Retrogression from Life. When the apostle Paul says that "through one man sin entered the world," he did not mean a man like ourselves; he was speaking of the Federal Head of the human race, the noble Being that God created. The third chapter of Genesis reveals how sin was introduced into the world. Watch the subtlety of Satan's reasoning: "And he said to the woman, 'Has God indeed said . . . ?' " The one thing he was aiming at was the dominion of God over man. "For God knows that in the day you eat of it, your eyes will be opened, and you will be like God, knowing good and evil"—that is, you will become God over yourself. Sin is not a creation, it is a relationship. The essential nature of sin is my claim to my right to myself.

When our Lord confronts men, He confronts them on that basis. Read the New Testament, and you will find that Jesus Christ did not get into a moral panic over the things that rouse us. We are staggered at immorality, but Jesus faced those things in the most amazingly calm way (see Matthew 21:31). When He was roused to a state of passionate indignation, it was by people who were never guilty of such things. What our Lord faced continually was the disposition behind either the morality or the immorality. "If I had not come and spoken to them, they would have no sin . . ." (John 15:22).

Any man would have known without His coming that it was wrong to take life; the law is written in him. Any man would have known that immorality was wrong. But no man apart from Jesus Christ would believe that "my right to myself" is the very essence of sin. When we realize what Jesus means when He says, in effect, "If you would be My disciple, give up your right to yourself to Me," we begin to understand that "the carnal mind is enmity against God." "I will not give up my right to myself; I will serve God as I choose." Jesus Christ came to remove this disposition of self-realization.

Readjustment into Life. Sin interrupted the normal development of man, and it required another Man to take up the story where it was broken off and to complete it, without the sin. "You have no life in you," said Jesus (John 6:53). What life? The life He had, the life that is at the true Source. Eternal life means the life Jesus lived. "And this is the testimony: that God has given us eternal life, and this life is in his Son" (1 John 5:11). Eternal life is the life Jesus lived, the life of God in a mortal being, transformed by God's regenerating power into harmony with Himself.

"In Him was life, and the life was the light of men" (John 1:4). Why did Jesus live thirty-three years if all He came to do was to die for sin? He lived thirty-three years because He had to show what a normal man after God's pattern was like. He died that through His death we might have the source of life that was in Him (Romans 5:17). That is why it is so absurd to say, "I accept Jesus as a teacher only." Try to apply the teachings of Jesus to your life without an understanding of His death, and you will find it cannot be done. It would either make you commit suicide or take you to the cross and give you an understanding of why it was necessary for Him to die.

Preaching about the life of Jesus awakens an immense craving, but it leaves us with the luxury of sympathy with ourselves. "Oh well, I know that is very high and holy, but I was not born that way and God cannot expect that kind of life from me." We like to hear about the life of Jesus, about His teaching and His works, about His sympathy and tenderness, but when we stand face-to-face with Him in the light of God and He convicts us of sin, we resent it. Men crave what the Gospel presents but they resent the way it is presented by Jesus. That is a point that has been lost sight of these days, and every now and again the Church succumbs to the temptation to which Jesus Christ did not succumb—the temptation of putting men's needs first, with the result that certain features of the Gospel are eliminated.

Never separate the incarnation and the atonement. The incarnation was not for the self-realization of God, but for the purpose of removing sin and reinstating humanity into communion with God. Jesus Christ became incarnate for one purpose: to make a way back to God, that man might stand before Him as he was created to do, the friend and lover of God Himself. The atonement means infinitely more than we can conceive; it means that we can be morally identified with Jesus Christ until we understand what the apostle Paul meant when he said, "it is no longer I who live, but Christ lives in me."

All the mighty efficacy of the death of Jesus, of His resurrection and ascension to the right hand of the throne of God, is implanted into us by regeneration. And the lowest and most sin-stained can go that way. The measure of the salvation of Jesus is not what it does for the best man we know, but what it does for the worst and most sin-stained. There is no son of man that need despair; Jesus Christ can reproduce His saving work in any and every man, blessed be the name of God! Do we know anything about the sublime innocence that is the outcome of regeneration, and are we developing along that line? Are we transforming innocence into holiness by a series of moral choices, or are we paying too much attention to the natural life? When we are rightly related to God as Jesus was, the spiritual life becomes as natural as the life of a child. The one dominant note of the life after sanctification is the simplicity of a child, full of the radiant peace and joy of God. "Unless you are converted and become as little children . . . ."

His Unrecorded Years and Our Hidden Life

The Unrecorded Years
His Physical Development
His Psychical Development (Luke 2:40)
His Personal Development
Our Unconscious Form
Our Subconscious Mind (Colossians 3:3)
Our Conscious Self

The Unveiled Year (Luke 2:40-52)
His Environment and Ours (Matthew 2:13-14, 19-21
His Intimates and Ours (Matthew 13:55-56; Mark 3:21;
Luke 2:51; John 7:5)
His Imaginations and Ours (Luke 2:49; Colossians 3:1-3)

The Unaging Youth
(John 8:58; Matthew 18:3-5)

The new birth is illustrated by the supernatural advent of our Lord, not by the birth of a child into the world. Just as our Lord came into history from the outside, so He comes into our human nature from the outside. Our new birth is the birth of the Son of God into our old human nature, and our human nature has to be transfigured by the indwelling life of the Son of God. Mary, the mother of our Lord, is the type of our natural human life, which at critical moments so misunderstands the aims and objects of the Son of God. It was so in the historic life of our Lord, and it is true in our own personal experience. We make the blunder of imagining that when we are born from above, we cease to be ordinary human beings, whereas we become much more ordinary human beings than we were before. Our human nature goes on all the time. All through the unrecorded years of our Lord's life, His ordinary human life was being lived; nothing is recorded simply because there is nothing to record. After our birth from above, there is a corresponding phase in our lives when the life of God goes on in the deep unconscious part of our lives, and there is nothing to record.

The new birth is not the working of a natural law. The necessity for being born again is indicative of a huge tragedy. Sin has made the new birth necessary; it was not in the original design of God. New birth does not refer simply to a man's eternal salvation, but to his being of value to God in this order of things.

The Unrecorded Years

> And the child grew, and became strong in spirit filled with wisdom; and the grace of God was upon him (Luke 2:40).

When a young life passes from early childhood into girlhood or boyhood, there is a new birth of the mind, and the boy or girl becomes interested in literature, in poetry, and usually in religion. But that is not spiritual new birth and has nothing to do with the working of the Spirit of God; it has to do with the ordinary natural development of the life. At this stage, great devotion to God and to Christian service may be manifested, and this is apt to be looked on as an evidence of the work of the Spirit of God, whereas it is the mere outcome of the natural life beginning to unfold itself in the process of development. These things always go together: physical development, an alteration in bodily organs, and mental, moral, and spiritual development. The boy or girl sees more purely and clearly than the man or woman. No man thinks so clearly at any time or is ever so thrilled as he is in his "teens." Generally speaking, thirty years of age is the age of maturity. Some reach maturity before thirty and some after, but at about thirty is the age at which all the bodily and personal powers are matured. Up to that age, or what is represented by that age, life is full of promise, of visions, of uncertainties and expectations; after that there is no more promise, no more vision, the life has to be lived now in accord with all the visions it has had. There is a stage in ordinary natural life when maturity is reached, and if it is not reached, someone is to blame. That is in the physical domain. In the spiritual domain, the passing of the years counts for nothing. When we are born from above, the Son of God is formed in us; it is not the passing of the years that matures His life in us, but our obedience.

The angel said to Mary, "The Holy Spirit will come upon you, and the power of the Highest will overshadow you; therefore, also, that Holy one who is to be born will be called the Son of God" (Luke 1:35). That is symbolic of what happens when the Holy Spirit overshadows us: Our natural life is made the mother of the Son of God. What have we done with Him? Has He grown and developed? Has He been nourished and looked after, or has He been buried? When God comes, does He find something dead in us instead of the real living Son of God? We have to nourish the life of the Son of God in us, and we do it by obedience; that is, by bringing our natural life into accordance with His life and transforming it into a spiritual life.

There is another element in this new life that is often overlooked: It is unconscious in its growth. When Jesus said, "Consider the lilies of the field, how they grow," He was referring to the new life in us. If we make His words apply to the natural life only, we make Him appear foolish. If we are born of God and are obeying Him, the unconscious life is forming in us just where we are. God knows exactly the kind of garden to put His lilies in, and they grow and take form unconsciously. What is it that deforms natural beauty? Too much cultivation—too much denominational teaching will deform beauty in the spiritual world. Our danger is to take the place of God in regard to the new life. Jesus said, "Disciple in My *name*," that is, in His nature. The new life is in Him, and we have to remember that it grows like the lily. The right atmosphere for the new life to grow in is exactly where our natural life is placed. The things we cannot touch are not things for us to pout over, but things for us to accept as God's providential order for us. As natural men, we are not inclined to like the things God makes. At certain stages of our life, we much prefer the friends we make to our God-made relations, because we can be noble with our friends; we have no past history with them. We cannot be noble with our relations, because they knew us when we were mean, and now when we are with them, we cannot put on the pretense; it won't work.

The new life must go on and take form unconsciously. God is looking after it. He knows exactly the kind of nourishment as well as the kind of disintegration that is necessary. Be careful that you do not bury the new life or put it into circumstances where it cannot grow. A lily can only grow in the surroundings that suit it, and in the same way, God engineers the circumstances that are best fitted for the development of the life of His Son in us. It is the unconscious form that is continually alluded to in the New Testament. We must allow plenty of time for God to develop that life.

We hear it asked, "What is the good of all this study and reading of the Bible? We get no 'change' out of it." Most of us want something to show for what we do. We are not interested in God's life in us but only in our life in God. We are not after the development of the unconscious life of the Son of God in us, but after the "small change" that enables us to say, "I did this and that." The life of the Son of God grows feebler in a life of that order.

Every mind has two storeys, the conscious and the unconscious. Most of what we hear passes out of our conscious mind into our unconscious mind, and we think we have forgotten it, but we have not. We never forget anything; we cannot always recall it when we want to, but that is a different matter. We forget nothing; it is there, although not in the conscious mind, and when certain circumstances arise, suddenly the thing we thought we had forgotten is there to our amazement right enough. This is exactly what Jesus said the Holy Spirit would do: "He will . . . bring to your remembrance, all things that I said to you," The Holy Spirit is forming the unconscious mind all the time, and as we "mop up" His teaching—simply take it in, not try to estimate it as we would mathematical study—we shall find God is putting in the right soil for His life to grow. Our one concern is to keep in the right atmosphere. Where we are actually is the Almighty's business, not ours. "Consider the lilies." Our Lord knows what to do with His own lilies; if we try to transplant them, they will die. We are in such a desperate hurry, but it is in the unrecorded years, the times we are apt to think are of no account, that we are developing most for the value of the Son of God. There is a time coming when He will give an unveiled year, as He did in the life of His Son, and show what has been going on all the time.

The Unveiled Year

And the Child grew and became strong in spirit, filled with wisdom; and the grace of God was upon Him. . . . And Jesus increased in wisdom and stature, and in favor with God and men (Luke 2:40-52).

In the temple, the child Jesus was astonished that even His mother did not understand what He was doing. The one thing in us that makes us misunderstand Jesus Christ is our "Mary" life, that is, our natural life.

God will bring us to an unveiled year, when we will realize how we have grown without knowing it; things have altered amazingly. For example, we go through a great personal crisis in our life with God, and we conjure up all kinds of imaginary difficulties as to how things are going to fit in now with this person and with that. But when we come up to the circumstances, there is no external crisis at all, only the revelation of the tremendous alteration that has gone on in us unconsciously. When a crisis does come, it reveals that a tremendous alteration has taken place in us, and if there is any astonishment, it is in the fact that those whom we thought would have understood us do not. Crises always reveal character. A great snare about crises is that we want to live for them. If we have had one great crisis in which the revelation has come of how wonderfully God has altered us, we will want another crisis. Most of our life is lived in ordinary human affairs, not in crises. It is

His Unrecorded Years and Our Hidden Life   49

comparatively easy for human nature to live in a big strain for a few minutes, but that is not what human nature is called upon to do. Human nature is called upon to live a life of drudgery. The intense awful crisis of, for instance, a war will be followed by years of drudgery from the lives that are left—shattered nerves, maimed men, and marred lives. We get our moments of light and insight when we see what God is after, and then we come to where there is no crisis but just the ordinary life to be lived. By and by God will give an unveiled year and reveal the wonder of what He has been doing in us all the time.

His Environment and Ours. "Now when they had departed, behold, the angel of the Lord appeared to Joseph in a dream, saying, 'Arise, and take the young Child and His mother, flee to Egypt, and stay there until I bring you word; for Herod will seek the young Child to destroy Him.' When he arose, he took the young Child and His mother by night and departed for Egypt . . ." (Matthew 2:13-14, 19-21). We each make our own environment; it is our personality that does it. Our Lord in His historic life came up against the providential order of tyranny, to which He submitted. He also met hatred and detestation and compromise, and He is born into the same kind of circumstances in our bodily lives. So beware of getting on the line of "Oh well, if only I had better circumstances." The circumstances of our Lord were anything but ideal; they were full of difficulties. Perhaps ours are the same, and we have to watch that we remain true to the life of the Son of God in us, not true to our own aims and ends. There is always a danger of mistaking our own aim and end from the aim of the life of God in us. Take it regarding the great subject of the call of God. The call of God is a call according to the nature of God; where we go in obedience to that call depends entirely on the providential circumstances that God engineers and is not of any moment. The danger is to fit the call of God into the idea of our own discernment and say, "God called me there." If we say so and stick to it, then it is good-bye to the development of the life of God in us. We have deliberately shifted the ground of His call to fit our own conception of what He wants.

The curse of much modern religion is that it makes us so desperately interested in ourselves, so arrogantly concerned about cleaning ourselves up. Jesus Christ was absolutely interested in God, and the saint is to be a simple, unaffected, natural human being indwelt by the Spirit of God. If the saint is paying attention to the source Jesus Christ, out of him and unconsciously to him are flowing the rivers of living water wherever he goes (see John 7:37-39). Men are either getting better or worse because of us.

His Intimates and Ours. "Is this not the carpenter's son? Is not His mother called Mary? And his brothers James, Joses, Simon, and Judas? And His sisters, are they not all with us? Where then did this Man get all these things?" (Matthew 13:55-56; see also Mark 3:21; Luke 2:51; John 7:5). These were the intimates our Lord grew up with in His own historic life. We say, "Oh, but the Lord must have had a sweet and delightful home life." But we are wrong. He had an exceedingly difficult home life. Jesus Christ's intimates were brothers and sisters who did not believe in Him, and He says that the disciple is not above his master (see Luke 6:40). Jesus Christ was a man among men, a man living in unsullied communion with God. That is the kind of man He expects us to be through His regeneration of us. He went down to Nazareth and "was subject to them." An amazing submission! The next time you feel inclined to grouse over uncongenial companions, remember that Jesus Christ had a devil in His company for three years.

Our Lord preached His first public sermon in the place where He was brought up, where He was most intimately known, and they smashed up His service and tried to kill Him. "Oh, but," we say, "I expected that when I was saved and sanctified, my father and mother and brothers and sisters would be made right, but instead they seem to be all wrong." If the mother of our Lord misunderstood Him, and His brethren did not believe in Him, the same things will happen to His life in us, and we must not think it strange concerning the misunderstandings of others. The life of the Son of God in us is brought into the same kind of circumstances that the historic life of Jesus Christ was brought into, and what was true of Him will be true also of His life in us.

It is not only our intimates who will misunderstand Him, but we ourselves. There is a good deal in our human nature that will not understand the life of the Son of God, that will say to Him, as His own mother did, "Now is Your time to work a miracle." The natural in us will always want the Son of God to work in our way. Jesus said, "Woman, what does your concern have to do with Me? My hour has not yet come," and Mary accepted the rebuke. Some of the things that belong to the life of the Son of God in us do not look sane or practical to the natural man. When Christ is formed in us by His regenerating power, our natural life experiences what Mary experienced: A sword we should never have known if we were not born of God, a type of suffering we should have known nothing about if the Son of God had not been formed in us. A sword had to go through the heart of Mary because of the Son of God, and because of the Son of God in us, a sword must go through our natural life, not our sinful life.

His Imaginations and Ours. "And He said to them, 'Why is it that you sought me? Did you not know that I must be about My Father's business?' " (Luke 2:49; see also Colossians 3:1-3). Our Lord was absolutely taken up with His Father; that was the inner state of His mind. To Jesus the earth was His Father's house, and His Father's concerns possessed His imagination. The teaching in the Sermon on the Mount is on this line. Jesus says, "Don't make the ambition of your life in accordance with your old human nature, but be the children of the Highest—put your concentration on the things of God." Jesus Christ is not simply making fine characters of virtuous men; His end and aim is that we may be the children of our Father in heaven (see Matthew 5:48).

Where is our imagination? In Colossians 3, we are told to set our affections on things above. That means concentration, and concentration is spiritual determination to fix the mind on the things of God. Don't say, "What shall I eat? What shall I drink?" but seek first the kingdom of God. "Oh yes, I did get born again, but . . ." "Yes, God did do something for me, but . . ." You will soon "but" the whole thing out and leave yourself as you were before. Jesus says, "Be anxious for nothing, fix your mind on Me, be carefully careless about everything except your relationship to Me." This will take time to do. When the unveiled year came, it revealed where our Lord's mind was, and He was amazed that His mother's mind was not there, too. "Did you not know that I must be about My Father's business?" It was the question of an amazed and wistful child who felt His mother should have understood. Neither have we any excuse for not understanding what Jesus Christ is after; when we are born again, we ought to know exactly why His life is born into us—for the glory of God.

His Unaging Youth

"Jesus said to them, 'Most assuredly, I say to you, before Abraham was, I AM' " (John 8:58; see also Matthew 18:3-5).

Spiritually we never grow old; through the passing of things we grow so many years young. The characteristic of the spiritual life is its unaging youth, exactly the opposite of the natural life. "I am . . . the First and the Last." The Ancient of Days represents the eternal childhood. God Almighty became the weakest thing in His own creation, a baby. When He comes into us in new birth, we can easily kill His life in us, or else we can see to it that His life is nourished according to the dictates of the Spirit of God, so that we grow "to the measure of the stature of the fullness of Christ." The mature saint is just like a little child, absolutely simple and joyful and lively. Go on living the life that God would have you live, and you will grow younger instead of older. There is a marvelous rejuvenescence when once you let God have His way. If you are feeling very old, then get born again and begin to grow in His new life.

The Silent Years to Thirty
Luke 2:40-52

A child's life has no dates; it is free, silent, dateless. A child's life ought to be a child's life, full of simplicity. By "the silent years to thirty," we mean to picture the experience of the sanctified soul. We have attained to nothing yet; we are simply perfectly adjusted to God. By sanctification we are placed in the condition of our Lord at Bethlehem, and we have the life of Jesus as our example. We are apt to mistake the sovereign works of grace in salvation and sanctification as being final; they are only beginnings.

His Evolution in Mind and Ours

We mean by evolution growth and development. In the child the body is put first ("And the Child grew"—v. 40); in the young man the mind is put first ("And Jesus increased in wisdom"—v. 52). During those silent years from twelve to thirty there is nothing recorded except that "Jesus increased in wisdom and stature, and in favor with God and men"— nothing precocious or enchanting, a slow, steady, sane progress till He reached maturity.

"Now Jesus Himself . . . [was] about thirty years of age" (Luke 3:23). That is the age from the Jewish standpoint at which physical maturity and soul maturity are supposed to be reached. Up to that age a man was looked on as almost a child and dependent; after thirty he was shielded from no requirements of a full-grown man. Up to the age of thirty life is full of promise and expectation. The powers are untried; they are more or less chaotic and immature. The majority of the works of genius are done before thirty. After thirty, or what is represented by that age, there is no more promise, no more vision; life has to be lived now in accordance with all the visions it has had.

Spiritual maturity is a different matter. Spiritual maturity is not reached by the passing of the years, but by obedience to the will of God. Some people mature into an understanding of God's will more quickly than others because they obey more readily; they more readily sacrifice the life of nature to the will of God; they more easily swing clear of little, determined opinions. It is these little, determined opinions, convictions of our own that won't budge, that hinder growth in grace and make us bitter and dogmatic, intolerant, and utterly un-Christlike.

Willing Zone. "Then he went down with them, and came to Nazareth" (v. 51). Will is not a faculty, but the whole man active. Our Lord sacrificed His own natural desire to the will of His Father. His natural desire would have been to stay in the temple, but "He went down with them and came to Nazareth," and stayed there eighteen years. This is an illustration of the way Jesus used His will all through His life (see John 6:38). He "increased in wisdom" by applying His will to the will of His Father. "For even Christ did not please Himself" (Romans 15:3). To do what we like always ends in immorality; to do what God would have us do always ends in growth in grace.

Wonder Zone. "Why is it that you sought me? Did you not know that I must be about My Father's business?"

(v. 49). This incident is the one glimpse given to us of those twelve years so full of wonder, so full of skylights open toward God. Think of the pure wonder of the child Jesus in the temple when He realized with spiritual intuition that He was in His Father's house. Don't picture a precocious intellectual prig. Jesus was amazed that His mother did not know what He knew or understand what He understood. A child's mind exhibits the innocence of intelligence, and in the life of Jesus this innocence never became conceited.

The starting point of every heresy is the corrupting of the innocence of intelligence by conceit. Conceit means to have a point of view; a point of view takes the wonder out of life. It is only when we are born again and sanctified that we enter into an understanding of the life of Jesus. His life is the kind of life that the Spirit forms in us when we obey Him, full of innocent wonder (see Matthew 11:25).

Waiting Zone. "Then He . . . was subject to them" (v. 51). Have we ever caught the full force of those ten days of waiting in the Upper Room? If we measure those periods by our modern way of estimating we will put it down as a waste of time; but into the life of our Lord, and into the lives of the early disciples, were going to come elements that would root and ground them on a solid foundation that nothing could shake.

The waiting time is always the testing time. How we hurry people into work for God! A thrilling experience, an ecstasy of spiritual emotion, a heavenly vision, and "I am called of God to preach"! Are you? Get back to God's Book. If you are called to preach, God will put you through mills you never dreamed of. To testify for God is absolutely essential, but never open your mouth as a preacher unless you are called of God. If you are, it is a "woe to me if I do not preach," not a delight.

One of the worst signs among us is that we are more interested in the most recent views on sanctification than we are in the testimonies in God's Book. Any excitable, hysterical testimony from a tide of revival is apt to be more welcome to the majority of sanctified people than the bedrock teaching of the New Testament. With what result? "... because they had no root, they withered away." Picture those silent years in the life of our Lord, shielded by His Father, until all the tremendous forces of His life were developed and grasped.

His Evolution in Body and Ours

Organic Soul. "And Jesus increased in . . . stature" (Luke 2:52). The spirit is soul expressing itself in the body. The body has an enormous influence on the soul, and the soul on the body. When the body is developing into manhood or womanhood, there is a sudden awakening of the soul to religious influences, and it is always a dangerous time. What is looked upon as evidence of the grace of God at work is merely the opening up of the soul in the process of development. God never places any importance on that phase.

Over and over again people have built up hope on the religious promise of boys and girls in their teens, and after a while when it fades away the unwise say that he or she has backslidden. May God have mercy on the parents who develop precocity in a child! Precocity is something that ought to be checked. We are apt to place our faith on the years when we are in the making, whereas lives ought to be allowed to develop along a right line to the point of reliability.

If this is true in the physical and psychical domain, it is much more so in the spiritual. There are stages in spiritual development when God allows us to be dull, times when we cannot realize or feel anything. It is one of the greatest mercies that we have those blank spaces, for this reason: that if we go on with spiritual perception too quickly, we have no time to work it out. And if we have no time to work it out, it will react in stagnation and degeneration.

"Work out what God works in"—work it out through your fingertips, through your tongue, through your eyes. Then, when it is worked out, God will flood your soul with more light. Beware of curiosity in spiritual matters (see 2 Corinthians 11:3). If once you begin to push God's restrictions on one side and say, "I wonder what this movement is; I wonder if I should have this or that experience," you may find yourself getting perilously near the condition of the Prodigal Son, taking the law into your own hands and going clean off at a tangent. Unless religious emotions spring from the indwelling grace of God and are worked out on the right level, they will always, not sometimes, react on an immoral level. The time when these dangers begin is in this stage of development.

It is a wonderful point of illumination that our Lord's soul was in a body like ours, and that for thirty silent years He exhibited a holy life through all the stages of development that our lives go through.

Organic Self-sacrifice. "I lay down My life . . . I lay it down of Myself" (John 10:17-18). Our Lord was referring to the power He has of self-sacrifice. Have we that power? Thank God we have. After sanctification we have the power to deliberately take our sanctified selves and sacrifice them for God. It is an easy business to be self-sacrificing in mind: "I intended to do this and that"—that is, I estimate what it is going to cost me. Paul says he not only estimated the cost, he experienced it: ". . . for whom I have suffered the loss of all things."

As you go on toward maturity, watch for the secondary paths through the meadows: "I have been so blessed of God here, this is where I ought to stay." Read the life of Jesus. He kept His eyes fixed on the one purpose His Father had for His life, which He calls "going up to Jerusalem," and we have to go with Him there. One of the greatest snares is the number of good things we might do. Jesus Christ never did the good things He might have done; He did everything He ought to do because He had His eyes fixed on His Father's will, and He sacrificed Himself for His Father. It is not done once for all; it can only be done once for always, day by day, day by day, the sacrifice of ourselves to the will of Jesus. Self-realization is gone and Christ-realization has come in.

Difficult? Nothing is ever attained in the natural world without difficulty, and the same thing applies in the spiritual world. How many of us have learned the ABCs of concentration? "This one thing I do" —our face set like a flint toward the purposes of God, not fanatically doing our duty, but going steadfastly on with the sacrifice of ourselves for Jesus as He sacrificed Himself for His Father.

Organic Spirit. "Father, into Your hands I commend My spirit" (Luke 23:46). All through the life of Jesus there is a clear realization of His authority over body, soul, and spirit. He matured to that authority in those silent years. "Oh," you say, "but Jesus was the Son of God." He said He was the Son of Man; that is, He exhibited what we are to be when we become sons of God, and if He "learned obedience by the things which He suffered," are we going to rebel because we have to go the same way?

What are we doing with our brains since we entered into the experience of sanctification? Are we allowing the Holy Spirit to get hold of this bodily machine until we construct an expression of the mind of Christ? The Spirit of Jesus is given to us in new birth, but we have not the mind of Christ until we form it. How our minds express themselves depends entirely on the way we use our brains. I mean by mind not the spiritual mind, but the mind as it expresses itself in the bodily life.

"But we have the mind of Christ." It is not true to say that God gives us our ideas; that notion is the starting point of all heresies. God never gave anyone their ideas. God makes a man use his ideas in order to convey His mind; otherwise responsibility is destroyed. "Glean your thinking," says Paul, and we have to do it by will. The Holy Spirit energizes the will to complete mastery of the brain. Don't be a mental wool-gatherer.

His Evolution in Maturity and Ours

". . . at about thirty years of age . . ."—the period of maturity. Who was it reached maturity? The Son of God as man—the maturity of all physical powers, all soul powers, all spiritual powers. And not until that point was reached did God thrust Him out into the three years of service. "I do always those things that are pleasing to my Father." When did Jesus learn that power? In those thirty silent years.

Can God say of us: "That soul is learning, line upon line, precept upon precept. It is not nearly so petulant and stupid as it used to be; it no longer sulks in corners; it no longer murmurs against discipline. It is getting slowly to the place where I shall be able to do with it what I did with My own Son"? What was that? God took His hands off, as it were, and said to the world, the flesh, and the devil, "Do your worst." But "He who is in you is greater than he who is in the world." God shielded His Son from no requirements of a son, and when we are rightly related to God He will not shield us from any requirements of sons.

In spiritual maturity all our powers are thoroughly adjusted into a calm poise, rightly balanced, and God can begin to trust us with His work. "If anyone loves me, he will keep My word," said Jesus. He is referring to the freedom of the disciple to keep His commandments. No natural man is free to keep the commandments of God; he is utterly unable to unless he is born again of the Holy Spirit. Freedom means the ability to keep the law; every kind of freedom has to be earned.

". . . and my Father will love him, and we will come to him, and make our home with him"—an unspeakable, not-able-to-be-stated communion, God the Father, God the Son and God the Holy Spirit, and the sinner saved and sanctified by grace, communing together. That is the sheer sovereign work of the Lord Jesus Christ.

His Baptism and Our Vocation

His Baptism
The Anticipations of John (John 1:26-34)
The Attitude of Jesus Himself (Mark 1:9-11)
The Acceptations of Jesus for Himself (Luke 3:21-23)
The Appointment of Jesus in Himself (Matthew 3:13-15)

Our Vocation
The Anticipations of God (Hebrews 2:9-10)
The Attitude of the Saint Himself (1 Corinthians 1:26-29)
The Acceptations of the Saint for Himself (Acts 20:24)
The Appointment of the Saint in Himself (Philippians 3:10)

The age of thirty represents the perfection of physical, mental, and spiritual powers. Jesus Christ was thirty years of age when He was baptized; all His powers were fully matured. For thirty years our Lord had done nothing in public; then at the preaching of John the Baptist He emerged and was baptized with the baptism of John, which is a baptism of repentance from sin. Our Lord's baptism is not an illustration of the Christian rite of baptism, nor of the baptism of the Holy Spirit. At His baptism, our Lord accepted His vocation, which was to bear away the sin of the world. We have no corresponding experience to that. Jesus Christ did not come to do anything less than to bear away the sin of the world: That is His vocation as Son of Man. By His bearing away the sin of the world, the way is opened up for every human being to get to God as if there had been no sin. The revelation in the Bible is not that Jesus Christ was punished for our *sins,* but that He took upon Him the *sin* of the human race and put it away—an infinitely profounder revelation (see 2 Corinthians 5:21; Hebrews 9:26). All through the Bible it is revealed that our Lord bore the sin of the world by *identification,* and not by *sympathy.* He deliberately took upon His own shoulders and bore in His own person the whole massed sin of the human race. Our Lord knew what He had come to do, and His baptism is the first public manifestation of His identification with sin, with a conscious understanding of what He was doing. At His baptism He visibly and distinctly and historically took upon Him His vocation.

The Anticipations of John. "John answered them, saying, 'I baptize with water, but there stands One among you whom you do not know. It is He who, coming after me, is preferred before me, whose sandal strap I am not worthy to loose . . . .' And John bore witness, saying, 'I saw the Spirit descending from heaven like a dove, and He remained upon Him. And I did not know Him, but He who sent me to baptize with water said to me, "Upon whom you see the Spirit descending, and remaining on Him, this is He who baptizes with the Holy Spirit." And I have seen and testified that this is the Son of God' " (John 1:26-34). The anticipations of John, which were built upon the Old Testament, begin to be fulfilled in our Lord's baptism (Matthew 3:10-12). Jesus Christ is the true baptizer; He baptizes with the Holy Spirit. He is the Lamb of God that takes away the sin of the world—my sin (see 1 John 2:1). He is the One who can make me like Himself; the baptism of John could not do that.

The Anticipations of God. "But we see Jesus, who was made a little lower than the angels, for the suffering of death crowned with glory and honor, that He, by the grace of God, might taste death for everyone. For it was fitting for Him, for whom are all things, and by whom are all things, in bringing many sons to glory, to make the author of their salvation perfect through suffering" (Hebrews 2:9-10). God's anticipations work in us because our Lord accepted His vocation. God anticipates that He is going to bring sons and daughters, not "saved souls," to glory. A saved soul is simply one who has partaken of the mighty efficacy of redemption. A son or daughter of God is one who has not only partaken of redemption, but has become of value to God in this order of things.

We must ever make a practical distinction in our minds between the revelation of redemption and the conscious experience of salvation. Redemption is absolutely finished and complete, but its reference to individual men is a question of their individual action. The whole human race is condemned to salvation by the cross of our Lord. God nowhere holds a man responsible for having the heredity of sin; the condemnation begins when a man sees and understands that God can deliver him from the heredity of sin and he refuses to let Him do it. At that moment he begins to get the seal of damnation. John 3:19 is the final word of condemnation: "This is the condemnation" (the critical moment), "that the light has come into the world, and men loved darkness rather than light, because their deeds were evil."

Is God realizing His anticipations in our lives? Is the Son of God reaching His maturity in us? The formation of the Son of God in us and our putting on of the new man must go together. We are brooded over by the Holy Spirit (Luke 1:35), and that which is formed in us is the Holy Son of God (Galatians 1:15-16). His life is formed in our human nature and it develops quietly in the unrecorded years. We live our ordinary life as human beings remembering that our natural life, although delivered from sin, is continually in danger of misunderstanding the Son of God, just as Mary misunderstood her own Son.

In a hundred and one ways, we can prefer that the sword should go through the Son of God in us rather than through our natural life, and that our natural impressions should have the ascendancy rather than the Son of God. The putting on of the new man means that we must not allow our natural life to dictate to the Son of God but see to it that we give Him ample chance to dominate every bit of us. He has delivered us from sin; now we must see that He dominates our natural life also until the life of Jesus is manifested in our mortal flesh.

This is the meaning of bringing a son or daughter to glory, and it is also the meaning of the efficacy of our Lord's baptism and the acceptance of His vocation being worked out in individual lives. Our Lord's vocation, which He accepted at His baptism, was His identification with sin. Our vocation is to fulfill the anticipations of God and to become His sons and daughters. The majority of us so harp on the ordinary evangelical line that we thank God for saving us and then leave the thing alone. We cannot grow *into* holiness, but we must grow in it. Are we accepting our vocation and determining to let the Son of God manifest Himself in our mortal flesh? If we are, it will mean that our human nature must be perfectly obedient to the Son of God and that we must bring all our imagination and fancies and thoughts into captivity to the obedience of Christ.

The Attitude of Jesus Himself. "It came to pass in those days that Jesus came from Nazareth of Galilee, and was baptized by John in the Jordan. And immediately coming from the water, He saw the heavens parting and the Spirit descending upon him like a dove. Then a voice came from heaven, 'You are My beloved Son, in whom I am well pleased' " (Mark 1:9-11). The baptism of our Lord was an extraordinary spiritual experience to Himself. "And there came a voice from heaven, saying, 'You are My beloved Son, in whom I am well pleased.' " We have no experience like that; it stands unique. There is only one beloved Son of God; we are sons of God through His redemption. John's baptism was a baptism of repentance from sin, and that was the baptism with which Jesus was baptized. He was baptized into sin, *made to be sin*, and that is why His Father was well pleased with Him. When our Lord took on Him His vocation as the sin-bearer, the Holy Spirit descended, and the voice of the Father came. The Holy Spirit descended on Him as a dove; He comes to us as fire. The descent of the Holy Spirit and the voice of the Father were to our Lord the seal on His accepted vocation.

The cross of Jesus Christ and His baptism express the same thing. Our Lord was not a martyr; He was not merely a good man; He was God Incarnate. He came down to the lowest reach of creation to bring back the whole human race to God, and to do this He must take upon Him, as representative man, the whole massed sin of the race. That is why He is called "the Lamb of God." It was in this connection also that God said, "You are My beloved Son." "Though he was a Son, yet he learned obedience by the things which he suffered." The Son of God alone can redeem, and because He was the Son of God, He became man that He might bring man back to God.

We so continually run down the revelations of the New Testament to the level of our own experience. That is wrong. We must let God lift up our experience to the standard of His Word.

The Attitude of the Saint Himself. "For you see your calling, brethren, that not many wise according to the flesh, not many mighty, not many noble, are called. But God has chosen the foolish things of the world to shame the wise, and God has chosen the weak things of the world to put to shame the things which are mighty; and the base things of the world and things which are despised God has chosen, and the things which are not, to bring to nothing the things that are, that no flesh should glory in His presence" (1 Corinthians 1:26-29). This is our calling as saints, and it is the only line on which the Holy Spirit will witness to us. He will never witness to our wits, or to our intelligence, or to our physical perfections, or to our insight or genius, or to anything at all that is natural to us. He will only witness to that which has been produced in us by His redemption. Are we watching our experience, or are we estimating the witness of the Holy Spirit? The Holy Spirit witnesses only to the Son of God, and not according to our fleshly estimates of things (2 Corinthians 5:16), and if we try to estimate Jesus Christ according to the flesh, we shall find there is no reality in it.

Spiritually, God always builds upon the weakest link, never on the strong link. The empires of the world were all founded on strong men; consequently, they broke because no chain is stronger than its weakest link. God Almighty became Incarnate as a helpless babe in Bethlehem, and Jesus Christ begins His life in us by a new birth. Do we realize that our human nature has to become the birthplace of the Son of God, or have we only realized the miracle of God's changing grace? "Bring up this child for me." How is the life of the Son of God growing in our bodily life? Are we putting on the new man in keeping with the Son of God born in us? How is the Son of God progressing in the affections of our heart and the imaginations of our mind?

Have we crushed Him ? The historic Son of God was put to death because the wits and wisdom of this world could not agree with Him, but blasphemed Him and crucified Him, and the same thing may happen in any individual life. Watch the barriers God puts into your life. The natural life says, "I ought to be this and that." But God has told you you cannot. Woe be to you if you hanker for a second after the thing about which God has said "No" to you. If you do, you will put to death the life of God in you. Are you willing to accept the barrier from Him? It may be a barrier with regard to personal ambition for His service. This must be our attitude to ourselves: fellowship with the things that are despised, the things that look ostensibly weak to the wise things of the world. They are not weak to God because they are based on His redemption. When we accept our vocation of sons and daughters of God, we become identified with the Son of God, who was Himself despised and rejected of men.

The Acceptations of Jesus for Himself. "Now when all the people were baptized, it came to pass that Jesus was baptized and while He prayed, the heaven was opened. And the Holy Spirit descended in bodily form like a dove upon Him, and a voice came from heaven which said, 'You are My beloved Son; in You I am well pleased.' Now Jesus Himself began His ministry at about thirty years of age, being (as was supposed) the son of Joseph, the son of Heli" (Luke 3:21-23). We read that Jesus was in communion with His Father at the time of His baptism: "Jesus also was baptized, and prayed." Our Lord accepted His vocation in the center of His spirit; consequently, the temptations, when they came, made no appeal to Him although they were based on amazingly wise strategy. Satan could not get near Him. The vocation our Lord had accepted was that of sin-bearer, not of dominating world-lord. Satan's aim was to get Him to fulfill His vocation on another line: "There is no need *to die* for sin, You can fulfill Your vocation by a 'short cut' and evade the cross." He came to redeem men, not to set them a wonderful example.

The Acceptations of the Saint for Himself. "But none of these things move me; nor do I count my life dear to myself, so that I may finish my race with joy, and the ministry, which I received from the Lord Jesus, to testify to the gospel of the grace of God" (Acts 20:24). "None of these things move me," says Paul. What things? The things that were to smash Paul's heart, crumple up his body, and extinguish all his earthly ambitions. Have we accepted that kind of vocation, or are we only concerned that we get deeply conscious communion with God? The acceptation of the saint for himself is that he is concerned about nothing at all except this one thing, "that I might finish my race with joy," not happiness. Joy is the result of the perfect fulfillment of what a person is created for. Happiness depends on things that happen and may sometimes be an insult. It is continually necessary to revert to what the New Testament asks us to accept about ourselves. Have we received this ministry from Jesus, "As You sent Me into the world, I also have sent them into the world"? How did the Father send Him? "For I have come down from heaven, not to do My own will, but the will of Him who sent Me." The first obedience of Jesus was to the will of His Father, not to the needs of men. Then our first accepted vocation is not to help men, but to obey God, and when we accept that vocation, we enter into relationship with the despised and the neglected. It is always easy to neglect a man or woman who deliberately accepts the aim of his life from the Lord Jesus.

Many of us are imitators of other people; we do Christian work because someone has asked us to do it. We must receive our ministry, which is to testify the gospel of the grace of God, from Jesus Christ Himself, not from other Christians. Paul determined to relate everything to Jesus Christ and Him crucified (1 Corinthians 2:2). "You may do what you like with my external circumstances, but you shall not deflect me by making me consider myself, I have only one end—to fulfill the ministry I have received of the Lord Jesus." Just as our Lord accepted His vocation and Satan could not turn Him from it, so we as children of God through His redemption have to accept our vocation and to fulfill the ministry we receive from Him. All the onslaught of Satan gathered round the Son of God to prevent Him from fulfilling His vocation, and Jesus says the same thing will happen to us. We must beware of affections, of imaginations, of successes, of practical work, of organizations—of everything and everyone that would deflect us for one second from Jesus Christ's purpose in our life. It will mean going "outside the camp," the camp that wants to dictate over the head of Jesus Christ, "bearing His reproach."

The Appointment of Jesus in Himself. "Then Jesus came from Galilee to John at the Jordan to be baptized by him. And John tried to prevent Him, saying, 'I have need to be baptized by You, and are you coming to me?' But Jesus answered and said to him, 'Permit it to be so now, for thus it is fitting for us to fulfill all righteousness' " (Matthew 3:13-15). John knew who Jesus Christ was—the One who was to baptize with the Holy Spirit and fire, and yet that One comes to him to be baptized with the baptism of repentance. No wonder John was amazed, and he refused to baptize Jesus until Jesus said, "Permit it to be so now, for thus it is fitting for us to fulfill all righteousness." John, as the forerunner of the Messiah, had no business to introduce his own conceptions as to what was fitting for the Messiah; John had to obey just as the Messiah did. The vocation of our Lord was His identification with sin: He became absolutely and entirely identified with sin, and His baptism is the sign before the whole world of the acceptance of His vocation. "This is what I am here for." It was not the baptism into power and dominion, but a baptism into identification with sin. The disposition of sin, for example, my claim to my right to myself, entered into the human race by one man (Romans 5:12), and the Holy Spirit entered into the human race by another Man, so that "where sin abounded, grace did abound much more." Jesus Christ by His death bore away the sin of the world, and by our identification with His death, we can be delivered from the heredity of sin and can receive a new heredity, the unsullied holiness of Jesus Christ. We receive this new heredity not by imitation, but by identification by giving up our right to ourselves to Jesus Christ (see Galatians 2:20).

The Appointment of the Saint in Himself. "That I may know Him, and the power of His resurrection, and the fellowship of His sufferings, being conformed to His death" (Philippians 3:10). It is one thing to recognize what God is doing with us, but another thing to deliberately accept it as His appointment. We can never accept the appointment of Jesus Christ and bear away the sin of the world; that was His work. But He does ask us to accept our cross. What is my cross? The manifestation of the fact that I have given up my right to myself to Him forever. Self-interest, self-sympathy, self-pity—anything and everything that does not arise from a determination to accept my life entirely from Him will lead to a dissipation of my life. How many of us have dispassionately and clearly looked at Philippians 3:10? Paul is not speaking poetically but expressing plain, blunt, simple, spiritual, heroic fact. "That I may know Him" (not what He can do, nor what I can proclaim that He has done for me), "and the power of His resurrection" (that I continually receive my life from Him by deliberate appointment on my own part), "and the fellowship of His sufferings" (that I enter determinedly into His relationship with things, which means going contrary to my natural intuitions); "being conformed to His death." It is appalling how few are willing to efface their natural nobility. Fasting from food is an easy business, but fasting in its true nature means to fast from everything that is good until the appointments of God in my soul are accepted. For instance, there are times when a preacher, if he is eloquent or poetical, must fast from his own conceptions of things until he has accepted the appointment of God for his life. The One who is being hit hardest is Jesus Christ. Those of us who should have been fasting in fellowship with His sufferings have been out on the "noble natural" line, and the sword that was thrust at Him we have not turned aside but have lashed into Him and been applauded for doing it. "Being conformed to His death" (that I may be identified with the things in which He has interests), "if by any means, I may attain to the resurrection from the dead" (that I may have a resurrection like His, not merely the resurrection of a saved soul, but of one who has proved himself a son of God by the redemption of our Lord).

Many of us are not living in the domain in which Christianity alone can be lived—the domain of deliberate identification with Jesus Christ. It takes time, and it ought to take time, and the time is not misspent for the soul who will wait before God and accept His appointment for his individual life.

The Self-Consciousness of Jesus—I
His Baptism

All things have been delivered to Me by My Father, and no one knows the Son, except the Father. Nor does anyone know the Father, except the Son, and he to whom the Son wills to reveal Him (Matthew 11:27).

There is a self-consciousness that is more or less of a disease, arising from unstrung nerves or from personal conceit. We cannot apply the term to our Lord in that sense. By the term *the self-consciousness of Jesus* is meant the state of His being conscious of His personal self. I would like to warn against the modern literature that says we can understand the self-consciousness of Jesus Christ by examining our own. Jesus says emphatically, "No one knows the Son, except the Father." Any teaching regarding the personality of Jesus that gives the lie to what He says about Himself is antichrist; it "dissolves by analysis" (see 1 John 4:1-3).

In attempting to deal with the self-consciousness of Jesus, we must remember that we are dealing with a revelation, something we do not have as natural men (although through the experience of regeneration we can have "the mind of Christ"; but the experience of new birth must take place first). "Let this mind be in you, which was also in Christ Jesus" (Philippians 2:5). "But we have the mind of Christ" (1 Corinthians 2:16).

In these studies, the birth of Jesus at Bethlehem stands for a presentation of the experience of sanctification in which the soul is put into a state of spiritual innocence before God, a state of untried, untested innocence. Then we have to develop that innocence into holiness by a series of moral choices whereby we sacrifice the life of nature to the will of God. The majority of us know only the experience of sanctification; we do not press on to transform innocence into holiness until all our powers are matured for God. Insubordination too often marks the beginnings of the sanctified life because we will not submit to the normal development that God demands. As soon as we enter the sanctified life, we expect we are going to be giants for God. We are in danger of becoming fanatical instead of developing along the great, sane, majestic lines on which Jesus developed.

The distinction between a saved soul and a disciple is fundamental. The stern conditions laid down by our Lord for discipleship are not the conditions of salvation; discipleship is a much closer, more conscious relationship (see Luke 14:26-27,33). The secret of discipleship is the cross of our Lord Jesus Christ (Galatians 6:14; see 1 Corinthians 2:2).

Just when maturity is reached spiritually we cannot say; all we know is, it depends entirely on obedience. After they were baptized with the Holy Spirit, the early disciples evidently reached the point of spiritual maturity, for we read that they were "rejoicing that they were counted worthy to suffer shame for His name." They could not be appealed to on any other line than the one marked out for them by Jesus; it could not be tyrannized or martyred out of them. The baptism of our Lord represents this point of amazing maturity; we are faced with a revelation we cannot understand, but must accept.

The Innate Realization of Jesus Himself
John 1:26-34

The experience of Jesus at His baptism is as foreign to us as His incarnation. Read the so-called "lives" of Jesus and see how little is made of His baptism, the reason being that most of the writers take the baptism to be something to teach us, or as an illustration of the rite of baptism. In the New Testament the baptism of Jesus is not taken as an illustration of anything that we experience; it is recorded as a manifestation of who Jesus was. He stands forth consciously—Son of God, Son of Man, God-Man—having come for one purpose; to bear away the sin of the world.

We have been dealing with our Lord's childhood, and with the silent years of which nothing is recorded. Now at His baptism He emerges, a full, outstanding personality with a tremendous maturity of power that never wilts for one moment. There was no ambiguity in our Lord's mind as to who He was, or as to the meaning of the step He was taking. He was no longer maturing; He was mature. He is not manifested here as our example, but as God incarnate, for one purpose— to be identified with the sin of the world and to bear it away.

Jesus fully felt Himself to be all that John the Baptist expected He would be. Take time to find out from the Old Testament what John did expect Him to be. Then realize that Jesus was consciously that; and you will understand why He said, "No one knows the Son, except the Father." The reason we have no counterpart in our experience of the baptism of Jesus is because of His innate realization of who He was. The Jesus of the New Testament is a Being who made Napoleon say, "I know men, and Jesus Christ is not a man." What he meant was that in Jesus Christ he had come across a preeminent Master of men.

The Extraordinary Revelation
Mark 1:9-11

Beware of bringing to the study of Jesus anything that does not belong to the New Testament. If we bring preconceived notions of our own, we shall never look at the facts. If we are being taught "as the truth is in Jesus," we shall accept the revelation that His baptism was an extraordinary experience to our Lord—extraordinary even to Him.

When Jesus came from Galilee to the Jordan to be baptized by John, it was a tremendous epoch in the purpose of God Almighty. Who among us could presume to say what Jesus experienced when He was baptized? Jesus came forth at the threshold of His public ministry in the full consciousness of who He was. From that moment, He manifested Himself as being here for one purpose only—to be identified with the sin of the world and to bear it away. "God was in Christ reconciling the world to Himself." Who was Jesus? God incarnate. Watch what He says of Himself: In effect, "I do not work from My right to Myself" (John 5:19, 30); "I do not think or speak from My right to Myself" (John 8:28; 12:49); "I do not live from My right to Myself (John 6:38); "I work and think and live from My Father's right to Me." "I delight to do your will, O my God."

The Enduement Regally
Luke 3:21-22

We read that Jesus was in communion with His Father at the time of His baptism ("Jesus also was baptized; and . . . prayed . . ."—an inconceivable communion). And what happened? ". . . heaven was opened. And the Holy Spirit descended in bodily form like a dove upon Him, and a voice came from heaven which said, 'You are My beloved Son; in You I am well pleased.' " It was a purely personal experience. The Holy Spirit descended upon Jesus, and the voice of the Father said to Him, "You are My beloved Son." This Man, who was known to men as the humble Nazarene carpenter, was almighty God presented in the guise of a human life.

"Opened heaven" to our Lord means opened heaven to everyone. The Holy Spirit descending as a dove is symbolic of the Holy Spirit life that Jesus can communicate to every person. The New Testament records two personal descents of the Holy Spirit: one on our Lord as Son of Man at His baptism, the other on the Day of Pentecost—"Therefore being exalted to the right hand of God, and having received from the Father the promise of the Holy Spirit, He poured out this which you now see and hear" (Acts 2:33). By right of His death and resurrection and ascension our Lord can impart the Holy Spirit to any and every person (Luke 11:33; John 20:22).

The Eminent Redeemer
Matthew 3:13-15

"Then Jesus comes from Galilee to John at the Jordan, to be baptized by him." What was John's baptism? The baptism of repentance for the remission of sins. Jesus was baptized by that baptism, not by a baptism like it. What did John regard Jesus as? "The Lamb of God, who takes away the sin of the world!" At His baptism Jesus took on Himself His vocation. It was the public manifestation that He became part of fallen humanity; that is why He was baptized with John's baptism of repentance.

Beware of saying that Jesus took on the sin of the human race by sympathy. It is being said today that Jesus had such a profound sympathy for the human race—that He was such a pure, noble character and realized so keenly the shame and horror of sin—that He took our sin on Himself by sympathy. All through the Bible it is revealed that our Lord bore the sin of the world by identification, not by sympathy. All I can say is: "Yes, I mourn over my sin and wrongdoing and I wish I were better. I do accept the life of Jesus as very beautiful and holy, but that holiness is not mine."

The New Testament says Jesus became identified literally with the sin of the human race. "He made Him who knew no sin"—here language almost fails—"to be sin for us," for one purpose only: "That we might become the righteousness of God in Him" (2 Corinthians 5:21). Repentance to be true must result in holiness, or it is not New Testament repentance. Repentance means not only sorrow and distress for the wrong done, but the acceptance of the atonement of Jesus that will make me what I have never been—holy.

Ask God to awaken in your heart and conscience a realization of what identification with sin on the part of Jesus meant. He did not come only to manifest what God was like; He came to put away sin by the sacrifice of Himself, so that men might see God in Him ("He who has seen me has seen the Father"). The manifestation of Jesus as God incarnate and in His holy manhood are incidents connected with the one great purpose of His coming, which was a vicarious identification with sin.

As saved and sanctified saints, have we ever realized that our vocation is a vicarious identification with the life of the world that is not right? One of the subtlest snares is the idea that we are here to live a holy life of our own, with our eyes fixed on our own whiteness. No, we are here to carry out God's will as Jesus carried it out. Jesus carried out the will of God as the Savior of the world; we are to carry out His will as saints. Jesus Christ was a vicarious sufferer for the sin of the world, and we have to be vicarious sufferers, filling up "that which is lacking of the afflictions of Christ." Have we ever realized that through the atonement we can take on ourselves a vicarious attitude before God, a vicarious penitence, knowing "the fellowship of his sufferings?"

Take it on the line of intercession. Have we ever realized that we can hold off the curse and the terror of evil and sin from people who do not know God? May God save us from the selfish meanness of a sanctified life that says, "I am saved and sanctified; look what a wonderful specimen I am." If we have been saved and sanctified, we have lost sight of ourselves absolutely. Self is effaced; it is not there. The sacrifice of the sanctified self is the lesson to be learned. We are saved and sanctified for God—not to be specimens in His showroom, but for God to do with us even as He did with Jesus, to make us broken bread and poured out wine as He chooses. That is the test—not spiritual fireworks or hysterics, not fanaticism, but a blazingly holy life that "confronts the horror of the world with a fierce purity," chaste physically, morally, and spiritually. And this can only come about in the way it came about in the life of our Lord.

Beware of the subtle insinuations that come in the guise of light, that we are to be like Jesus in the sense of sharing in His great mediatorial work. We are not. Jesus Christ came into the world to deliver humankind from sin; we do not. He was God incarnate; we are not. Jesus said that He came to do the will of His Father, and that He sends us to do His will. "As my Father has sent me, even so send I you." What is the will of Jesus? That we make disciples, after we ourselves have become disciples.

The emphasis today is being put on the fact that we

have to save people; we have not. We have to exalt the Savior who saves people, and then make disciples in His name. Jesus says, "I, if I am lifted up from the earth, will draw all people to Myself." If I lift up Jesus where the New Testament lifts Him up, on the cross—that is, if I present Him as being made sin and putting it away by the sacrifice of Himself—then Jesus says He will draw all men unto Him, and there will come the surprising illumination of the Spirit. ". . . so is everyone who is born of the Spirit." The *so* refers to the infinite surprise of the Spirit of God at work in the souls of men bringing the amazing revelation, "I know who Jesus is." We have unconsciously usurped the place of the Holy Spirit; we present a series of argumentative doctrines and say, "If you believe this and accept that, something will happen." It never happens in that way, but always as a tremendous surprise.

The touchstone of the Holy Spirit's working in us is the answer to our Lord's question: "Who do men say that I, the Son of Man, am?" Our Lord makes human destiny depend on that one thing, who men say He is, because the revelation of who Jesus is is given only by the Holy Spirit. The sign that we have received the Holy Spirit is that we think rightly of Jesus. Jesus bases membership in His church on the revelation of who He is: "You are the Christ, the Son of the living God." That is the rock on which Jesus builds His church—that is, the revelation of who He is and the public confession of it (see 1 Corinthians 7:3).

His Temptation and Ours

Hebrews 2:18; 4:15-16

The Isolation of Mastership (Matthew 4:1-2)
His Watch in Faith (Matthew 4:3-4)
His Wait in Hope (Matthew 4:5-7)
His Way of Love (Matthew 4:8-10)
The Limit to the Devil (Matthew 4:11)

The Inner Martyrdom (1 Peter 4:12-13)
Our Lure of Wits (Matthew 11:6)
Our Light of Wisdom (John 12:16)
Our Liberty of Wonders (Luke 17:21)
The Limit to Temptation (1 Corinthians 10:13)

Temptation is not sin; we are bound to meet it if we are human. Not to be tempted would be to be beneath contempt. Temptation is a suggested short cut to the realization of the highest at which we aim. The way steel is tested is a good illustration of temptation. Steel can be "tired" in the process of testing, and in this way its strength is measured. Temptation is the testing by an alien power of the possessions held by a personality so that a higher and nobler character may come out of the test.

This makes the temptation of our Lord explainable. He held in His own person His unspotted sanctity and the fact that He was to be the King of men and the Savior of the world, and Satan was the alien power that came to test Him on these lines. The period of temptation came immediately after one of spiritual exaltation (see Matthew 3:16-17; 4:1). It was a period of estimating forces, and the records reveal how our Lord faced and rejected the visions of a swift fulfillment of His vocation presented to Him by Satan. Jesus Christ in His baptism had accepted His vocation of bearing away the sin of the world, and soon He was put by God's Spirit into the testing machine of the devil. But He did not "tire," He retained the possessions of His personality intact. He was tempted, "yet without sin."

The temptations of our Lord have no home at all in our human nature; they do not appeal to us because they are removed from any affinity with the natural. Our Lord's temptations and ours move in different spheres until we become His brethren, by being born again (see Hebrews 2:11). The temptations of Jesus are not those of man as man, but the temptations of God as man. The statement that our Lord was tempted as ordinary people are is readily accepted, but the Bible does not say that He was so tempted. Jesus Christ was not born with a heredity of sin; He was not tempted in all points as ordinary people are but tempted like His brethren, those who have been born from above by the Spirit of God and placed in the kingdom of God by supernatural regeneration.

The records of our Lord's temptations are given not that we might fathom Him, but that we might know what to expect when we are regenerated. When we are born again of the Spirit of God and enter into fellowship with Jesus Christ, then the temptations of our Lord are applicable to us. We are apt to imagine that when we are saved and sanctified, we are delivered from temptation; we are not, we are loosened into it. Before we are born again, we are not free enough to be tempted, neither morally nor spiritually. As soon as we are born into the kingdom of God, we get our first introduction into what God calls temptation—the temptations of His Son. God does not shield any man or woman from the requirements of a full-grown man or woman. The Son of God is submitted to temptations in our individual lives, and He expects us to remain loyal to Him (see Luke 22:28). The honor of Jesus Christ is at stake in our bodily life. Are we remaining loyal to the Son of God in the things that beset His life in us? The personality of a saint holds all that God intends a man or woman to be, and the temptation to him comes along the line it came to our Lord—to fulfill what his personality holds on a line other than God intends.

The Isolation of Mastership

> Then Jesus was led up by the Spirit into the wilderness to be tempted by the devil. And when he had fasted forty days and forty nights, afterward He was hungry (Matthew 4:1-2).

The Spirit of God drove our Lord into the wilderness for one purpose—to be tempted of the devil, and not only to test Him, but to reveal what Christian mastership means.

In that isolation the Lord Jesus Christ met the strong man and overcame him and bound him, and he gives us "power . . . over all the power of the enemy." The writer to the Hebrews does not say, "When you are tempted, imitate Jesus." He says, "Go to Jesus, and He will succor you in the nick of time." That is, all His perfect overcoming of temptation is ours (see Hebrews 2:18).

The Bible reveals that man is related to the historical

introduction of Satan. The communication between man and the devil, resulting in the fall, has meant that God does not deal with Satan directly. Man must deal with Satan. Satan is to be overcome and conquered by human beings. That is why God became incarnate. It is in the incarnation that Satan is overcome.

The Inner Martyrdom

Beloved, do not think it strange concerning the fiery trial which is to try you, as though some strange thing happened to you: but rejoice to the extent that you partake of Christ's sufferings, that when His glory is revealed, you may also be glad with exceeding joy (1 Peter 4:12-13).

In the history of the church, inner martyrdom and external martyrdom have rarely gone together. We are familiar with external martyrdom but inner martyrdom is infinitely more vital. Paul deals with it in Philippians 2. "Christ Jesus . . . made Himself of no reputation" (that is, He annihilated by His own deliberate choice all His former position of glory) "taking the form of a servant." If we are to be in fellowship with Him, we must deliberately go through the annihilation, not of glory, but of our former right to ourselves in every shape and form. Until this inner martyrdom is gone through, temptation will always take us unawares. Peter says, "Beloved, do not think it strange concerning the fiery trial which is to try you." The internal distresses are accounted for by the fact that the saint is being taken into an understanding of what our Lord went through when He was driven by the Spirit into the wilderness to be tempted. Satan tried to put Jesus Christ on the way to becoming King of the world and Savior of mankind in a way other than that predetermined by God. The devil does not tempt us to do wrong things; he tries to make us lose what God has put into us by regeneration—the possibility of being a value to God. When we are born from above, the central citadel of the devil's attack is the same in us as it was in our Lord; that is, to do God's will in our own way.

His Watch in Faith. "Now when the tempter came to Him, he said, 'If You are the Son of God, command that these stones become bread.' But He answered and said, 'It is written, "Man shall not live by bread alone, but by every word that proceeds from the mouth of God" ' "(Matthew 4:3-4). In each of the three never-to-be-forgotten pictures that our Lord has given us, the temptation of Satan centers round this point: "You are the Son of God, then do God's work in Your own way; assert Your prerogative of Sonship." The first temptation was to set up a selfish kingdom. "You are the Son of God, then command these stones to be made bread; You do not need to be hungry; satisfy Your own needs and the needs of men, and You will get the kingship of men." Was Satan right? Read John 6:15: "Jesus perceived that they were about to come and take Him by force to make Him king." Why? He had just fed five thousand of them! It must have been a dazzling vision that Satan presented to our Lord, for who could ever have such sympathy with the needs of men and women as He? For one impressive moment He must have wondered. But our Lord would not be king of men on that line. "But He answered and said, 'It is written, "Man shall not live by bread alone, but by every word that proceeds from the mouth of God." ' " He deliberately rejected the suggested "short cut," and chose the "long, long trail," evading none of the suffering involved.

In His temptation our Lord does not stand as an individual man; He stands as the whole human race vested in one personality, and every one of us when regenerated can find his place and fellowship in those temptations.

Our Lure of Wits. "And blessed is he who is not offended because of Me" (Matthew 11:6). The deep dejection of John is the dejection of a great man (Matthew 11:11). John's misgivings arose from the fact that the wonderful things God had told him about the Messiah, whom he foreran, seemed to be without application to Jesus Christ (Matthew 3:11-12). It was a case of wits versus revelation.

The first temptation of our Lord comes to us on this line: "Be sensible, You are here for the service of men, and surely it is the most practical thing to feed them and satisfy their needs." The clamor abroad today is all on this line: "Put man's needs first; never mind about the first commandment, the second commandment is the all-important one" (see Mark 12:29-31). This advice sounds sensible and right, but at its heart is the temptation of Satan to put men's needs first. The insistent demand in the world today to put people's needs before God's will is the outcome of the reasoning of human wits and wisdom, and who can say that the demand is a wrong one? So long as our wits and human solutions are on the throne, to satisfy the needs of men is ostensibly the grandest thing to do. Every temptation of Satan will certainly seem right to us unless we have the Spirit of God. Fellowship with our Lord is the only way to detect them as being wrong.

The conditions of our civilized life today ought to be realized more keenly by the Christian than by the natural person. But we must see that the worship of God is put on the throne and not our human wits. The evidence of

Christianity is not the good works that go on in the world; these are the outcome of the good there is in human nature, which still holds remnants of what God designed it to be. There is much that is admirable in the civilization of the world, but there is no promise in it. The natural virtues exhaust themselves; they do not develop. Jesus Christ is not a social reformer; He came to alter us first, and if any social reform is to be done on earth, we will have to do it. Social reform is part of the work of the ordinary honorable humanity, and a Christian does it because his worship is for the Son of God, not because he sees it is the most sensible thing to do. The first great duty of the Christian is not to the needs of his fellowmen, but to the will of his Savior. We have to remember the counsel of our Lord, given from the center of His own agony, "Watch and pray, lest you enter into temptation." Keep steadfastly true to what you know is God's order and listen to no suggestions from elsewhere. The one thing that will keep us watching and praying is continuing to worship God while we do our duty in the world as ordinary human beings.

His Wait in Hope. "Then the devil took Him up into the holy city, set Him on the pinnacle of the temple, and said to Him, 'If you are the Son of God, throw yourself down. For it is written: "He shall give His angels charge concerning you," and, "In their hands they shall bear you up, lest you dash your foot against a stone." ' Jesus said to him, 'It is written again, "You shall not tempt the Lord your God" ' " (Matthew 4:5-7).

This temptation presents a wild reach of possibility: "You are the Son of God, then fling Yourself off the pinnacle of the temple; do something supernatural; use signs and wonders and bewitch men, so that they will be staggered out of their wits by amazement, and the world will be at Your feet. Set up a spectacular kingdom." Our Lord never once used signs and wonders to get a person off his guard and then say, "Now believe in Me." Jesus Christ never coerced anybody. He never used supernatural powers or the apparatus of revival. He refused to stagger human wits into submitting to Him. He always put the case to a person in cold blood: "Take time and consider what you are doing" (see Luke 9:57-62). Jesus Christ is engaged in making disciples in the natural sense; consequently, He never entrances a person by rapture or enamors him out of his wits by fascination. Instead, He puts Himself before a man in the baldest light conceivable: "If you would be My disciple, these are the conditions" (see Luke 14:26-27, 33). A person must believe in Jesus Christ by a deliberate determination of his own choice. The temptation to the church is to go into the "show business." Our Lord told His disciples they would be witnesses unto Him, a satisfaction to Him wherever they were placed (see Acts 1:8).

Our Light of Wisdom. "His disciples did not understand these things at first; but when Jesus was glorified, then they remembered that these things were written about Him and that they had done these things to Him" (John 12:16). Our Lord's temptations are carefully presented, so that we may know the kind of temptation to expect when His life is formed in us. This second temptation is apt to come with tremendous lure after the experience of sanctification: "Now that I am saved and sanctified, God will surely turn the world upside down and prove what a wonderful thing He has done in me. Every unsaved soul will be saved, every demon-possessed man delivered, and every sick person healed." "You will easily get Your kingship of men if You will use signs and wonders and stagger men's wits," said Satan to our Lord. And the same temptation comes to the church and to individual Christians. It sounds right to ask God to produce signs and wonders, and throughout the twenty centuries of the Christian era, this temptation has been yielded to, every now and again, in the most wild and inordinate manner. Unfortunately, this has also occurred in the tongues movement, and hundreds of those who were really enlightened by the Spirit of God have gone off on the line of this temptation.

We are apt to have the idea that we can only estimate what God is in us by what He does through us. What about our Lord and Master, what did He do? The marvelous thing about Him is what He did not do. Think what an ignominious failure His life was, judged from every standpoint but God's. Our Lord did not say that signs and wonders would not follow but that the one set purpose for us is that we do God's will in His way, not in our way. All the wisdom seems to be with the temptations, but our Lord by the light of the Holy Spirit reveals where they are wrong. Are we prepared to continue with the Son of God in His temptations in us, or are we going to betray Him and say, "Now that I am saved and sanctified, I must expect God to do wonders"? It sounds right and wise, and it commends itself to our natural wisdom if once we forget our Lord's counsel to watch and pray.

His Way of Love. "Again, the devil took Him up on an exceedingly high mountain, and showed Him all the kingdoms of the world and their glory. And he said to Him, 'All these things I will give You, if You will fall down and worship me.' Then Jesus said to him, 'Away with you,

Satan! For it is written, "You shall worship the Lord your God, and Him only you shall serve" ' " (Matthew 4:8-10).

Our Lord was then asked to compromise: "You will become the King of men and the Savior of the world by judicious compromise; build Your kingdom on broad-minded lines. You know there is evil in the world; then use it wisely, and don't be so intense against sin. Don't talk about the devil and hell. Don't be so extreme and say a person needs to be born from above. Tolerate my rule of the world, call things 'necessary evils.' Tell people sin is not anarchy, but a disease. Fall down and worship me and my way of looking at things, and I will withdraw and the whole world will be yours. Establish a socialistic kingdom." The first sign of the dethroning of Jesus is the apparent absence of the devil, and the peaceful propaganda that is spread after he has withdrawn. Will the church that bows down and compromises succeed? Of course it will, it is the very thing that the natural man wants. This line of temptation as revealed by our Lord is the most appallingly subtle of all.

Temptation yielded to is lust deified. In the Bible, the term "lust" is used of other things than merely of immorality. It is the spirit of "I must have it at once; I will have my desire gratified, and I will tolerate no restraint." Each temptation of our Lord contains the deification of lust: "You will get the kingship of the world at once by putting men's needs first. Use signs and wonders, compromise with evil, judiciously harmonize with natural forces, and you will get the kingship of men at once." At the heart of every one of our Lord's answers are these words: "For I have come down from heaven, not to do My own will, but the will of Him who sent Me" (John 6:38); that is, "I came to do God's work in His way not in My own way, although I am the Son of God."

The temptation to woo and win people is the most subtle of all, and it is a line that commends itself to us naturally. But you cannot woo and win a mutiny; it is absolutely impossible. You cannot woo and win the one who when he recognizes the rule of God detests it. The gospel of Jesus Christ always marks the line of demarcation; His attitude throughout is one of sternness, there must be no compromise. The only way in which the kingdom of God can be established is by the love of God as revealed in the cross of Jesus Christ, not by the lovingkindness of a backboneless being without justice or righteousness or truth. The background of God's love is holiness. His is not a compromising love, and the kingdom of our Lord can only be brought in by means of His love at work in regeneration. Then when we are regenerated, we must not insult God by imagining that in dealing with our fellowmen, we can afford to ignore the need for redemption and simply be kind and gentle and loving to all.

Our Liberty of Wonders. "Nor will they say, 'See here!' or, 'See there!' For indeed, the kingdom of God is within you" (Luke 17:21). "The kingdom of God is within you," uncompromisingly within you. We must never compromise with the kingdoms of this world; the temptation the devil presents is that we should compromise. We recognize his temptation in the teaching that proclaims there is no such being as the devil and no such place as hell; much that is called sin is a mere defect; men and women are like poor babes lost in the wood, just be kind and gentle with them, talk about the fatherhood of God, about universalism and brotherhood, the kindness of Providence and the nobility of man. Our Lord's temptations reveal where the onslaught will come. Today, through an overabundance of Christian activities, Jesus Christ is being dethroned in hearts, and Christian wits and wisdom are taking His place; consequently, when trials and difficulties come, most of us are at our wits' end because we have succumbed to one or another of these temptations.

The Limit to the Devil. "Then the devil left Him, and behold, angels came and ministered to Him" (Matthew 4:11). The sign of victory is that the temptation has been gone through successfully. If our Lord had failed in any degree, the angels would have had no affinity with Him. The affinities of a man after a period of temptation prove whether he has yielded to it or not. The practical test for us when we have been through a season of temptation is whether we have a finer and deeper affinity for the highest. Temptation must come, and we do not know what it is until we meet it. When we do meet it, we must not debate with God but stand absolutely true to Him, no matter what it costs us personally, and we will find that the onslaught will leave us with higher and purer affinities than before.

The Limit to Temptation. "No temptation has overtaken you except such as is common to man; but God is faithful, who will not allow you to be tempted beyond what you are able, but with the temptation will also make the way of escape, that you may be able to bear it" (1 Corinthians 10:13). God does not keep us from temptation; He supports us in the middle of it. Temptation is not something we may escape; it is essential to the full-orbed life of a child of God. We have to beware lest we think we are tempted as no one else is tempted. What we go through is the common inheritance of the race, not something no one ever went through before. It is most humiliating to be taken off our pedestal of suffering and made to realize that thousands of others are going though the same thing as we are going through.

Under the three pictures presented by our Lord, every temptation of the devil is embraced. We must ever remember the counsel of our Lord to watch and pray lest we enter into temptation. Prayer is easy for us because of all it cost the Son of God to make it possible for us to pray. It is on the basis of His redemption that we pray, not on the basis of our penetration or of our wits or understanding.

The Self-Consciousness of Jesus—II
His Temptation (Matthew 4:1-11)

In the silent years our Lord learned how to be; at His baptism He had revealed to Him what He had to do; in the temptation He learned what to avoid. Always remember that what is exhibited in the life of our Lord is for our instruction when once we have been readjusted to God through the atonement.

"Then Jesus was led up by the Spirit into the wilderness to be tempted by the devil" (v. 1). Immediately after His baptism Jesus was driven by the Spirit (not by the devil) into the wilderness to be tempted of the devil. The Spirit submitted Jesus to the tremendous onslaught of a supernatural being next to God in power. We talk much too glibly about the devil. If our Lord was led into temptation, it behooves us not to rush into it. "Resist the devil," not attack him. Our Lord taught us to pray, "Lead us not into temptation." When once we know that we are stronger through testing, the danger is real to seek it.

"And He was there in the wilderness forty days, tempted by Satan, and was with the wild beasts" (Mark 1:13). It was not because Jesus spent forty days in solitude that He was strong, but because of the power that He matured in the wilderness, living not by earthly but by heavenly law. Solitude is bad unless the life is driven there by God. "Whosoever delighteth in solitude is a wild beast or a god," wrote Plato. Solitude may come after God's supreme call, as it came to the apostle Paul (see Galatians 1:15-16), but the main characteristic of Christianity is to drive us out of solitude. Other religions earn it as a reward.

The word temptation is built on a Latin word meaning "to stretch." Every nature brings the setting of its own temptation; it is the thing held that is strained. If you are not holy, you will not be tempted to be unholy, because you do not hold holiness. Temptation is no temptation at all if it is clearly to evil. "God cannot be tempted by evil," says James, "nor does He Himself tempt anyone." But as soon as we come to man—and in the case of our Lord, the Son of God incarnate as Man—temptation is possible. He "was in all points tempted as we are, yet without sin."

Temptation is the test by an alien power of the possessions held by a personality. What did Jesus hold? He held in His person His own unspotted sanctity and the fact that He was to be the King of men and the Savior of the world; and the Spirit of God drove Him into the wilderness to be tested and strained on these points. Steel can become "tired" in the process of testing, and in this way its strength measured. Everything on earth, animate and inanimate, can be fatigued; but Satan could not begin to fatigue our Lord; He retained the possessions of His personality intact.

The affinities of a man after a period of temptation prove whether or not he has yielded. ". . . and behold, angels came and ministered to Him." If Jesus had failed in any degree, the angels would have had no affinity with Him. It was in the temptation that Jesus met the strong man and overcame him (Luke 11:21-22). It was in the temptation that our Lord bruised the head of the serpent (Genesis 3:15; see also Romans 16:20). Every temptation of Satan is perfectly wise. The wisest, shrewdest, most subtle things are said by Satan, and they are accepted by everybody as the acme of human philosophy. But when the Spirit of God is at work in a person, instantly can be seen the hollow mockery at the heart of what Satan is trying to do. When we understand the inwardness of the temptation, we see how Satan's strategy is turned into confusion by the Spirit of God.

The Possibility of the Public Ministry (vv. 1-4)

If You are the Son of God, command that these stones become bread (v. 3).

Jesus Christ came to be the Savior of the world and the King of mankind. No one could ever have such an understanding of the condition of people or of their needs as He had. Now watch what Satan says: "Put people's needs first. Heal their bodies, give them bread, and they will crown You King. Your chance is symbolized in Your own particular need. Satisfy Your own requirements first, and then the needs of every other person." Was Satan right?

Read John 6:15. After He had fed the five thousand, the temptation was repeated, but "When Jesus perceived that they were about to come and take Him by force to make Him king, He departed again to a mountain by Himself alone." He would not realize His kingship of men along that line.

What is the attitude of the church today? Christ on the throne of God? No, man on the throne of God! The tendency is to reverse the order of the commandments (see Mark 7:29-31). The temptation that beset our Lord with such fascination and power is the very temptation besetting the modern Christian: "Heal bodies, cast out demons, feed the poor, and men will crown You King."

The temptation is more powerful today than it has ever been in the history of the church—to put people's needs first, not God; to spell God in the term humanity; to make God an et cetera for blessing humanity. If you heal people and give them bread, what do they care about the claims of Jesus Christ? Health and happiness is what is wanted today and Jesus Christ is simply exploited. We who name the name of Christ, are we beginning to discern what Satan is after? He is trying to fatigue out of us what God has put in—that is, the possibility of being of value to God. Our only safety is to watch our Lord and Savior. "For in that He Himself has suffered, being tempted, He is able to aid those who are tempted" (Hebrews 2:18).

The Possibility of Powerful Mastery
(vv. 5-7)

If you are the Son of God, throw yourself down . . .
(v. 6).

Remember that temptation, literally, is to try the strength of the thing held. Satan did not tempt Jesus to sin, as we think of sin; he knew better. The one thing Satan aims at is that we put ourselves as master instead of God (see Genesis 3:5). And now he comes to the Son of God and says, "You are the King and the Savior of mankind; why not use Your power? Use apparatus. Startle people out of their wits and then say, 'Believe in Me.' " Could Jesus Christ have manifested His mastery over people in that way? Of course He could. But the Son of God as Son of Man is showing what a normal holy man is like. At His baptism our Lord accepted His vocation to bear away the sin of the world, and in this place of absolute loneliness He is being tested by all the powers that are against God; yet He went through the temptation without fatigue.

There are plenty of Christians today who are not appealed to on the "bread line," but the "signs and wonders" line does appeal to them. What is the cunning thing that is rending the church today? Where it is not socialism, it is supernaturalism: "Ask God for manifestations to prove you are a child of His." Satan's one aim is to thwart God's purpose and he can do it easily if he succeeds in making us take this line: "Now that I am baptized with the Holy Spirit, there must be marvelous manifestations that will amaze people at what God has done for me." Jesus said, "When He, the Spirit of truth, has come, . . . He will glorify Me"—not glorify you.

The error of the "signs and wonders" movement is that the eye is fixed not on Jesus, but on our own whiteness, or on the amazing of those around us because of what God has done. Jesus Christ never went on that line, and the unobtrusive kind of life He lived is exactly the kind of life the saints are to live. There was no "show business" with the Son of God, and there is to be no "show business" with the saints.

". . . do you think that I cannot now pray to My Father, and He will provide Me with more than twelve legions of angels?" (Matthew 26:53). Why did Jesus refuse supernatural intervention? It was not His Father's will for Him; that is the only reason. "How then could the Scriptures be fulfilled, that it must happen thus?" "He was crucified through weakness"—the strongest Being who ever trod this earth, because He knew what He could do and did not do it. "He saved others; Himself he cannot save." Think of the miserable little "struts" we exhibit—"I must insist on my rights." Then take them! But if you are a saint, you have a glorious opportunity of following the example of Jesus and being strong enough to decline to exercise your rights.

An infallible sign of error spiritually is when all you can say about a man or woman of God is that he or she is so sweet, so beautiful, so gentle; he or she has never been true to the Lord. If the Holy Spirit is indwelling a man or woman, no matter how sweet, how beautiful, how Christlike they are, the lasting thought you go away with is—What a wonderful Being the Lord Jesus Christ is!

The Possibility of Political Messiahship (vv. 8-11)

All these things I will give You, if You will fall down and worship me (v. 9).

This is the most subtle temptation of all: "You are the Son of God; You are here to fulfill all the promises of God; and You know perfectly well that if You compromise judiciously with the powers of evil, You can easily overcome them and will pull the whole world around to Your flag." Is Satan right? He certainly is. The first sign of the dethronement of God is the apparent absence of the devil and the peaceful propaganda that is spread abroad. The great cry today is, "Be broad. Accommodate yourself with evil so diplomatically that the line of demarcation is gone. Run up the white flag. Say to the prince of this world, 'We have been too puritanical in the past; there has been too clear a division between us. Now we will go arm-in-arm.' "

Is that the order? Never! "And the devil said to him, 'All this authority I will give You, and their glory; for this has been delivered to me, and I give it to whomever I wish' "

(Luke 4:6). Satan is the prince of this world, and during this dispensation he has power to give authority to those who will yield to him and compromise. We are here to stand true to God, not to attack people. No prophet ever lived by his message; as soon as he tries to, he must accommodate his message to the standards of the people. The messenger of God has to stand where Jesus Christ stood, steadfast in obedience to God first. One of the most curious phases today is that people are expecting the devil to do things. Let us keep our eyes on God, and remember that behind the devil is God, and that the Son of God has bruised Satan's head.

There is a wonderful symbolism about the place of the crucifixion: Jesus was crucified at "a place called Golgotha, that is to say, Place of a Skull." That is where He has always been put to shame, in the thinking part of man; and only when the thinking part of a man is swayed by the Holy Spirit will he find an answer to every one of the temptations that Satan brings. The temptation to the first Adam was to ignore the supremacy of God over the individual, to make man his own god. What was it Satan tried to make the last Adam do? To do God's will according to His own discernment: "You are the Son of God; assert Your prerogative of Sonship."

Jesus was led into the wilderness to see whether what He held in His Person—that is, His unique Saviorhood and His unspotted sanctity—would stand the test. The first Adam did not stand the strain for very long, but the last Adam did not begin to give way under the strain. Adam was innocent, not holy—that is, he had no wrong disposition in him; yet he was tempted. Jesus was holy, yet He was tempted. It was impossible to tempt Jesus with evil. The first obedience of Jesus was not to the needs of people but to the will of His Father, and at the heart of every one of our Lord's answers is this: "I came to do God's work in His way, not in My own way, though I am the Son of God."

When we are sanctified we get our first introduction to what God calls temptation—that is, the temptation of His Son. We imagine that when we are sanctified we are delivered from temptation. We are not. We are loosened into it; we are not free enough before to be tempted. As soon as we are sanctified, we are free, and all these subtleties begin to work. God does not shield us from any requirements of a full-grown man or woman, because His aim is to bring many "sons to glory": not emotional, hysterical people, but men and women who can withstand and overcome and manifest not only innocence, but holiness.

We cannot be innocent in the sense that the first Adam was until we are remade by regeneration; and we cannot be holy in the sense that the last Adam was holy until we are made one with Him. Then the same temptations that betook our Lord will betake us when we have become His brethren (Hebrews 2:11).

His Transfiguration and Our Secret

Our Lord's Attitude (Luke 9:28)
Prayer always transfigures
The Attitude of the Disciples (Luke 9:32)
The natural must sleep
Our Lord's Aspect (Luke 9:29)
Preincarnate Glory
The Aspect of the Disciples (Luke 9:32).
Face to Face with Reality
Our Lord's Attendants (Mark 9:4)
Converse with the Glorified
The Attention of the Disciples (Luke 9:32)
They saw His glory and His companions
Our Lord's Attention (Luke 9:31)
His Death the Theme of Glory
The Amazement of the Disciples (Mark 9:5-6)
Hysterical Suggestions
Almighty God's Ascription (Luke 9:35)
God Incarnate
The Awe of the Disciples (Luke 9:34)
God's Word

As has been already stated, Christian psychology is not the study of human nature Christianized, but the endeavor to understand the wonder and the mystery of "Christ in you, the hope of glory." Jesus Christ must ever be profoundly more than we can fathom, but we must study Him to get to know the characteristics of the new life that is to be manifested in our mortal flesh.

The apostle John does not allude to the transfiguration in his gospel, yet his gospel is written from that standpoint, the standpoint of the exceeding majesty of the Lord Jesus Christ.

According to the revelation of the Bible, our Lord is not to be looked upon as an individual man, but as the One who represents the whole human race. At His baptism, our Lord accepted His vocation as sin-bearer, the Holy Spirit descended upon Him as Son of Man, and the voice of God came with the divine approval. And at the transfiguration, the voice of God came again. The baptism and the transfiguration reveal who our Lord is, and the secret of the Christian is that he knows the absolute deity of Jesus Christ.

The transfiguration occurs practically in the center of our Lord's earthly ministry. The fulfillment of the transfiguration is the ascension. These two mountain peaks, without the cross and the resurrection, would portray the development of human life had there been no sin. The cross and the resurrection deal with sin and the need of redemption.

Our Lord's Attitude

And it came to pass, about eight days after these sayings, that he took Peter, John, and James and went up on the mountain to pray (Luke 9:28).

In our Lord's presentation, prayer is the point where the reality of God merges with human life. Until we are born from above, prayer with us is honestly nothing more than a mere exercise. But in all our Lord's teaching and in His own personal life, as well as in the emphasis laid on prayer by the

Holy Spirit after He had gone, prayer is regarded as *the* work (see John 14:12-13). Prayer in the Son of God as Son of Man is amazingly significant. If prayer is the highest reach of communion possible between almighty God and the Son of Man, what part ought prayer to play in our lives? Prayer with us often becomes merely a way of patronizing God. Our Lord's view of prayer is that it represents the highest reach possible to a man or woman when rightly related to God, perfectly obedient in every particular and in perfect communion with Him. Prayer is not meant to develop us, but to develop the life of God in us after new birth.

The Attitude of the Disciples

But Peter and those with him were heavy with sleep (Luke 9:32).

The natural must sleep. If we are ever going to know who the Lord Jesus Christ is, we must be born from above into another kingdom and discern by a power other than our natural wits. The natural is not sinful, but the natural is not spiritual. When the redemption of God has dealt with sin and delivered from it, then the natural must be sacrificed. Simeon said to the mother of Jesus, "Yes, a sword will pierce through your own soul also," but not because of sin. Mary was the natural mother of the Son of God, and in that wonderful experience of the incoming of the Son of God into the human race, she stands for our human nature. The natural has to be transfigured and subordinated to the spiritual; it must not force itself.

It was required of Adam—the federal head of the human race—that he should turn his natural life into a spiritual life by obedience. That is, he was to have dominion over the life in the air and in the earth and in the sea, but he was not to have dominion over himself; God was to have dominion over him, and as he obeyed God, his natural life would be turned into a spiritual life. Adam represented what Jesus Christ represents; that is, the whole human race. If Adam had obeyed and transformed his innocence into holiness by a series of moral choices, the transfiguration of the human race would have happened in due course. But Adam disobeyed, and there entered in the disposition of sin, the disposition of self-realization: I am my own God. This disposition may work out in a hundred and one different ways, in decorous morality or in indecorous immorality, but it has the one basis: my claim to my right to myself. That disposition was never in our Lord. Self-will, self-assertiveness, self-seeking were never in Him. When we become rightly related to God, we are not simply put back into the relationship Adam was in, but into a relationship Adam was never in; we are put into the body of Christ, and then God does not shield us from any of the requirements of sons.

We have the notion at first that when we are saved and sanctified by God's supernatural grace, He does not require us to do anything, but it is only then that He begins to require anything of us. God did not shield His own Son; not only did He not shield Him, but He allowed Him to be driven into the wilderness to be tempted of the devil. After the baptism of Jesus and the descent of the Holy Spirit upon Him, God took His sheltering hand off Him, as it were, and let the devil do his worst. So after the work of sanctification, when the life of a saint really begins, God lifts His hand off and lets the world, the flesh, and the devil do their worst, for He is assured that "greater is He who is in you, than he who is in the world."

The trouble comes when we forget that the Son of God is born into our old human nature. Whether we are six years old or sixty, our human nature is thousands of years old. Jesus Christ says that His Father makes His revelations not to the virtues of human nature, not to the astute wisdom accumulated by the ages, but to "babes." Our Lord's words can only be understood by those who are born from above, and He reveals Himself only to such. The church of Jesus Christ is built on these two things: the divine revelation of who Jesus Christ is, and the public confession of it (see Matthew 16:13-19).

Our Lord's Aspect

> And as he prayed, the appearance of His face was altered, and His robe became white and glistening (Luke 9:29).

Our Lord had emptied Himself of His glory for the purposes of the incarnation, and the transfiguration reveals His glory again. The subliminal nature of Jesus was absolute deity, and it was that subliminal nature, the glory He had with the Father before the world was, that suddenly burst through on the Mount of Transfiguration and gave the manifestation of God and man in perfect oneness: In His Son, God became His own incarnation. The apostle John is insistent that any tendency to dissolve the person of Jesus by analysis is antichrist (see 1 John 4:1-3). It is this preincarnate glory that is being dissolved today. The test of any teaching is its estimate of Jesus Christ. The teaching may sound wonderful and beautiful but watch lest it have at its center the dethroning of Jesus Christ.

The Aspect of the Disciples

> And when they were fully awake, they saw His glory and the two men who stood with Him (Luke 9:32).

The disciples were with Jesus Christ on the mount, and in his epistle, Peter records what they saw there. He says "we . . . were eyewitnesses of His majesty" (2 Peter 1:16). Jesus Christ is no comrade to Peter, He is absolute King of Kings. In the Apocalypse, the apostle John gives the same revelation of the appalling and sublime majesty of Jesus Christ. The disciples are fully awake now and face-to-face with reality.

Intellectual thinking and reasoning never yet got a person to reality, because these are instruments of life, and not of the life itself. Our only organ for getting at reality is conscience, and the Holy Spirit always deals with conscience first. Intellect and emotions come in afterward as the instruments of human expression.

The disciples came down from the mount into the demon-possessed valley, but it was not until after the cross and the resurrection that they began to understand what they had seen, the reason being that what they had seen in vision on the mount had to be worked out into actual experience in their lives. By the presence of the Holy Spirit in us, we know who the Lord Jesus is. We know Him "after the Spirit." The Holy Spirit glorifies the Lord Jesus to us and in us until we know who He is and know the exceeding majesty of Him who said, "All power is given to me in heaven and in earth." We do not know this by our intellect or by our sensible reasoning, but by the real witness of the Paraclete of God. The eyes of the disciples needed to be opened by the impartation of quickening life from our Lord after the resurrection before they knew Him (see Luke 24:16, 31). And the only way in which we can know our Lord is by His Spirit.

Our Lord's Attendants

And Elijah appeared to them with Moses, and they were talking with Jesus (Mark 9:4).

Jesus was standing in the full blaze of His preincarnate glory while the two representatives of the Old Covenant talked with Him about the issue that He was about to accomplish at Jerusalem. Then He turned His back upon that glory, and came down from the mount to be identified with fallen humanity, symbolized by the demon-possessed boy. Had He gone back into the glory that was His before the incarnation having only reached the Mount of Transfiguration, He would have left the human race exactly where it was; His life would only have been a sublime ideal and nothing more: "His teachings are so fine. We do not need to have anything to do with the atonement or with those crude doctrines of the apostle Paul's about the cross and personal apprehension; it is quite enough for us to have the Sermon on the Mount." I should think it was! If Jesus Christ came to be an example only, He is the greatest torturer of the human race. But our Lord did not come primarily to teach us and give us an example; He came to lift us into a totally new kingdom and to impart a new life to which His teachings would apply.

The Attention of the Disciples

And when they were fully awake, they saw His glory
and the two men who stood with Him (Luke 9:32).

The disciples were eyewitnesses and earwitnesses of all that transpired on the mount. There is a curious insistence in the records on the fact that our Lord at His transfiguration and in the Garden of Gethsemane took His disciples to be witnesses of things that they could never experience. We see one reason why Jesus took them in Peter's epistles and in John's gospel. The Christian faith must stand in an almighty Christ, not in a human being who became divine.

Our Lord's Attention

> Who appeared in glory and spoke of His decease which He was about to accomplish at Jerusalem (Luke 9:31).

The visitors on the mount talked to Jesus in all His majesty and glory of almighty God, but they spoke of His death, not of His glory. Does not that seem an appalling anticlimax? The whole of their attention is centered on the death of the Lord Jesus. The word "death" has the meaning of "issue." They spoke of the issue He was about to accomplish at Jerusalem by His death—the historic manifestation of the redemption of the human race.

The redemption of the human race does not necessarily mean the salvation of every individual. Redemption is of universal application, but human responsibility is not done away with. Jesus Christ states emphatically that there are possibilities of eternal damnation for the person who positively neglects or positively rejects His redemption.

Jesus Christ emptied Himself of His glory a second time; He came down from the Mount of Transfiguration and accomplished His death at Jerusalem, for what purpose? That any individual of the human race might go straight to the heart of God without the slightest fear because of what Jesus did on the cross. This is the great effective working of redemption in human experience. Our Lord's death is not the death of a martyr; it is the exhibition of the heart of God, broken to bring the whole human race back into perfect oneness with Himself.

The death of Jesus is the only entrance into the life He lived. We cannot get into His life by admiring Him or by saying what a beautiful life His was, so pure and holy. To dwell only on His life would drive us to despair. We enter into His life by means of His death. Until the Holy Spirit has had His way with us spiritually, the death of Jesus Christ is an insignificant thing, and we are amazed that the New Testament should make so much of it. The death of Jesus Christ is always a puzzle to unsaved human nature. Why should the apostle Paul say, "For I determined not to know anything among you except Jesus Christ, and Him crucified"? Because unless the death of Jesus has the meaning the apostle Paul gave to it—that it is the entrance into His life—the resurrection has no meaning for us either. The life of Jesus is a wonderful example of a perfect human life, but what is the good of that to us? What is the good of presenting to us a speckless holiness that is hopeless of attainment? It would simply tantalize us. Unless Jesus Christ can put a totally new heredity into us, there is no use asking us to think about the wonderful life He lived. The revelation made by the redemption is that God can put into us a new disposition whereby we can live a totally new life.

Now we can see why our Lord lived the life He did for thirty-three years. Before He made the entrance into that life possible for any human being, He had to show us what the life of God's normal man was like. The life of Jesus is the life we have to live here, not hereafter. There is no chance to live this kind of life hereafter: We have to live it here. Our Lord's death is not the death of a martyr, not the death of a good man; His cross is the cross of God whereby any human being can enter into a totally new life. The way into the life of Jesus is not by imitation of Him, but by identification with His cross. That is the meaning of being born from above: We enter into His life by its entering into us.

We talk about imitating Jesus, but isn't it highly absurd! Before we have taken three steps, we come across lust, pride, envy, jealousy, hatred, malice, anger—things that never were in Him, and we get disheartened and say there is nothing in it. If Jesus Christ came to teach the human race only, He had better have stayed away. But if we know Him first as Savior by being born again, we know that He did not come to teach merely: He came to make us what He teaches we should be; He came to make us children of God. He came to give us the right disposition, not to tell us that we ought not to have the wrong one; and the way into all these benedictions is by means of His death.

To Christianize human nature is simply to veneer that which is not real. The life of Jesus Christ is the standard, and we receive His life by means of His death. The emphasis on His death is explained when we remember that His teaching only applies to His life in us. When we preach Christ, it is not His birth that we preach, but His cross, and we bring ourselves face-to-face with the wonder and power of His resurrection life.

The Amazement of the Disciples

> Then Peter answered and said to Jesus, "Rabbi, it is good for us to be here; and let us make three tabernacles: one for You, one for Moses, and one for Elijah"—because he did not know what to say, for they were greatly afraid (Mark 9:5-6).

Peter knew not what to say, then why did he say it? Have you never said things you should not have said? If we get a great grasp in vision of who Jesus is and try to work it out in our ordinary human life by the energy of the flesh, we shall do what Peter did: talk nonsense through sheer bewilderment. When we come to Peter's epistles, there is nothing hysterical about them. Peter has gone through disillusionment about himself; he has gone through seeing the death of his Lord and through identification with His death; through the experience of the receiving from the risen Lord the gift of the Holy Spirit, and he says, "We were not hysterical, we were eyewitnesses of His majesty when we were with Him in the holy mount."

Repeatedly the vision of entire sanctification, or of the baptism of the Holy Spirit, is mistaken for the actuality. The only test of the actuality is when we are brought down into things as they are; it is then that the reality must manifest itself. When Jesus had healed the demoniac boy, the disciples asked Him, "Why could we not cast him out?" So Jesus said to them, "This kind does not go out except by prayer and fasting"—by spiritual concentration on Him. We can ever remain powerless, as were the disciples, by trying to do God's work through ideas drawn from our own temperament instead of by concentration on His power.

Never mistake the wonderful visions God gives you for reality, but watch, for after the vision you will be brought straight down into the valley. We are not made for the mountains; we are made for the valley. Thank God for the mountains, for the glorious spiritual realization of who Jesus Christ is; but can we face things as they actually are in the light of the reality of Jesus Christ? Or do things as they are efface altogether our faith in Him and drive us into a panic? When Jesus said, "I go to prepare a place for you," it was to the cross He went. Through His cross He prepared a place for us to "sit with him in the heavenly places, in Christ Jesus" now not by and by. When we get to the cross, we do not go through and out the other side. We abide in the life to which the cross is the gateway; and the characteristic of the life is deep and profound sacrifice to God. We know who our Lord is by the power of His Spirit; we are strongly confident in Him, and the reality of our relationship to Him works out all the time in the actualities of our ordinary life.

Almighty God's Ascription

Then a voice came out of the cloud, saying, "This is My beloved Son. Hear Him!" (Luke 9:35).

It is the same voice that spoke at our Lord's baptism. God emphatically states, "This is My beloved Son": This Man, known to men as the humble Nazarene carpenter, is almighty God presented in the guise of a human life; "hear Him." How many of us do hear Him? We always hear the things we listen for, and our disposition determines what we listen for. When Jesus Christ alters our disposition, He gives us the power to hear as He hears.

The Awe of the Disciples

A cloud came and overshadowed them; and they were fearful as they entered the cloud (Luke 9:34).

When the clouds around are dark and terrible, thank God, the saints know that they are but "the dust of His feet," and when they fear as they enter into the cloud, they see "no man any more, except Jesus only with themselves."

The Transfiguration

The Great Divide

The Great (or Continental) Divide is the name given to the ultimate height of land in the Rocky Mountains where the waters separate and run one way to the Atlantic, the other to the Pacific. The Mount of Transfiguration is the Great Divide in the life of our Lord.

Toward the Summit
Matthew 16:13-17:8

When holy character was fully matured in our Lord, earth lost its hold on Him and He was transfigured. In all probability, if Adam had transformed his innocence into holy character by obeying God's voice, transfiguration would have been the way out of this order of things; there would have been no death. The entering in of sin made that impossible. "Therefore, just as through one man sin entered the world, and death through sin, and thus death spread to all men, because all sinned" (Romans 5:12). "For the wages of sin is death" (Romans 6:23).

Adam was intended by God to partake in his own development by sacrificing the life of nature to the will of God, and in that way to transform innocence into holiness. Our Lord came on the same plane as Adam and did all that Adam failed to do: He transformed innocence into holy character. And when He had reached the full purpose of His manhood, He was transfigured.

The characteristic of the holiness of almighty God is that it is absolute; it is impossible to antagonize or strain it. The characteristic of the holiness of Jesus is that it manifested itself by means of antagonism; it was a holiness that could be tested (see Hebrews 4:15). The Son of God as Son of Man transformed innocence into holy character bit by bit as things opposed; He did not exhibit an immutable holiness, but a holiness of which we can be made partakers—"that we may be partakers of His holiness" (Hebrews 12:10).

Jesus Christ revealed what a normal man should be and in so doing showed how we may become all that God wants us to be. When we are sanctified we do not get something like a landslide of holiness from heaven; we are introduced into a relationship of oneness with God. and as our Lord met antagonistic forces and overcame them, so must we. The life Jesus lived is a type of our life after sanctification. We are apt to make sanctification the end; it is only the beginning. Our holiness as saints consists in the exclusive dedication to God of our powers.

One thing that is not sufficiently noticed is the place of the transfiguration in the life of our Lord; it came at the climax of His public ministry. In Matthew 16 we read that Jesus asked His disciples, first, "Who do men say that I, the Son of Man, am?" and then, "But who do you say that I am?" In a flashing revelationary movement of discernment Peter confessed, "You are the Christ, the Son of the living God." Then our Lord laid down the basis of membership in His church: ". . . on this rock"—that is, the revelation of who Jesus is and the public confession of it—"I will build my church."

"From that time Jesus began to show to His disciples that He must go to Jerusalem, and suffer many things from the elders and chief priests and scribes, and be killed, and be raised again the third day." Our Lord had made mystical allusions to His death earlier (see John 2:19-22), but the disciples did not know what He meant. Here He tells them plainly why He came—to be killed. And now we read that He took three of the disciples into a high mountain apart, "and [He] was transfigured before them."

Another thing we are apt to overlook is what led up to the transfiguration in our Lord's own life. The gospels reveal three things—First, Jesus Christ's deliberate, free submission of Himself to His Father: "I can of myself do nothing." Second, the subordination of His intelligence to His Father: "The words that I speak to you, I do not speak on my authority." Third, the submission of His will (not the subjugation of His will) to His Father: ". . . the Father who dwells in Me, does the works."

All through, Jesus manifested a strong personal identity, but the dominant note was the submission of it all to His Father. He separated His holy self for God's purposes: "For their sakes I sanctify myself." Before He spoke, He listened with the inner ear to His Father; He never allowed thought to originate from Himself. "For I have not spoken on My own authority; but the Father who sent Me gave me a command, what I should say and what I should speak." That is the meaning of communion: an intelligent, determined submission. "Most assuredly, I say to you, the Son can do nothing of Himself, but what He sees the Father do." When we are sanctified, our spiritual education goes along the same lines—the deliberate sacrifice to God of the self God has sanctified; the determined subordination of our intelligence to God; and the determined submission of our will to God.

What a glorious opportunity there is for Jesus Christ in

our lives! We testify to salvation and sanctification, but are we proving day by day that Jesus Christ is "made to us sanctification" in all holy living, in all holy speaking, and in all holy thinking? Are we doing the "greater works" that Jesus said we should do because our wills are submitted to Him as He submitted His will to His Father?

Transformation on the Summit

And as he prayed, the appearance of his face was altered, and his robe became white and glistening (Luke 9:29).

We say, "No cross, no crown." In the life of our Lord, the crown of the glory of the transfiguration came before the cross. You never know Jesus Christ, and Him crucified, unless you have seen Him transfigured in all His transcendent majesty and glory; the cross to you is nothing but the cross of a martyr. If you have seen Jesus glorified, you know that the cross is the revelation of God's judgment on sin; that on the cross our Lord bore the whole massed sin of the human race. "He made Him who knew no sin to be sin for us." No wonder we say,

Since mine eyes have looked on Jesus
I've lost sight of all beside.

Have we seen Him "crowned with glory and honor"?

When the transfiguration took place, our Lord as the Son of Man had fulfilled all the requirements of His Father for His earthly life, and was back in the glory that He had with the Father before the world was. Why did He not stay there? Supposing Jesus had gone straight to heaven from the

Mount of Transfiguration. What would have happened? He would have gone alone. No one would ever have been able to follow Him; His life would have been only a glorious ideal to lash humanity to despair. If Jesus Christ had gone to heaven from the Mount of Transfiguration we might have worshiped Him, but we would have had no power to live the kind of life He lived.

But Jesus did not come to show us what a holy life was like; He came to make us holy by means of His death. The only way in which our Lord becomes our example is when His life has been imparted to us. When we partake of His life through the experience of regeneration, we are put into a state of innocence toward God, and we have then to do what Jesus did—transform that innocence into holy character by a series of moral choices.

All that transpired in the life of our Lord after the transfiguration is altogether vicarious; we are without a guide to it in our own experience. Up to the transfiguration we can understand His holy life and follow in His steps when we have received the Holy Spirit. After the transfiguration there is no point of similarity; everything is unfamiliar to us. Jesus Christ has a consciousness about which we know nothing. We have come to the place where He is completing the will of God for the salvation of fallen humanity.

Beware of the teaching that Jesus Christ suffered because He was so noble, so pure, so far beyond the age in which He lived, that men put Him to death. It is not true. No martyr ever said what He said: "I lay down my life by myself." As workers, you will find that people like to listen as long as you talk about the holiness of Jesus and exalt Him as a marvelous character; but as soon as you speak of His death and say that He became identified with sin that we might be delivered from it, you find resentment. In the New

Testament, everything centers in the cross. The cross did not happen to Jesus; He came on purpose for it.

Transition from the Summit
Luke 9:30-43

> Then behold, two men talked with Him . . . [They] spoke of his decease which He was about to accomplish at Jerusalem (vv. 30-31).

They spoke not of His glory, but of His death. Who were the glorified visitants? One was Moses, whom the rabbis said died of the embraces of God: God kissed him into eternity, an ecstasy of divine delight. The other visitant was Elijah, who was taken up to heaven in a mighty whirlwind with the accompaniment of horses and a chariot of fire, a marvelous ecstasy. Here on the Mount our Lord Jesus Christ was back in His preincarnate glory, and what did He do? He turned His back on the glory and came down from the Mount into the demon-possessed valley to be identified with sin on the cross.

The Bible is full of anticlimaxes. Over and over again we are brought up to a sublime height and then rushed down to earth. But this is an anticlimax no human mind could have dreamed of. The Son of God was transfigured before His disciples. We were "eyewitnesses of His majesty," says Peter in his epistle. The voice of the Father came with the divine approval: "This is My beloved Son, in whom I am well pleased. Hear Him." Then He came down from the Mount and was crucified in obscurity. At His baptism our Lord took upon Himself His vocation—that is, to take away the sin of the world by identification—and from the transfiguration onward, He fulfills that vocation. Between the baptism and the transfiguration no mention is made of Jesus Christ being made sin; during that time He was perfecting holiness, living the kind of life God requires us to live. After the transfiguration we see Him dealing with sin; He "put away sin by the sacrifice of Himself."

The completion of the transfiguration is the ascension, not the resurrection. The transfiguration is a glimpse of glory—but not yet. "For the Holy Spirit was not yet given, because Jesus was not yet glorified" (John 7:39).

We find here an explanation of why God sends His servants into difficult places after the experience of sanctification: He sends them where He sent His Son. Transfiguration is the necessary result of obeying God, and there are moments when the glory does shine through. But we have to come down into all that is symbolized by the demon-possessed valley, into the toil and turmoil of the world for His sake. The church of Jesus Christ is in danger of forgetting this nowadays; she is seeking favor in the eyes of the world, seeking signs and wonders, and Christ stands outside the door knocking.

Have you ever caught a glimpse of what going "outside the camp, bearing his reproach" means? What camp? The camp that does not put Jesus first. After the glorious vision in the heavenlies—what? "Fill up in my flesh what is lacking of the afflictions of Christ." Few of us get there because we stop short at sanctification. The emphasis is put on the subjective side. "Can Jesus Christ make me holy?" The dominant note with the apostle Paul was not sanctification, but Jesus Christ, and Him crucified. When we are baptized with the Holy Spirit, self is effaced in a glory of sacrifice for Jesus and we become His witnesses. Self-conscious devotion is gone, self-conscious service is killed, and one thing only remains: Jesus Christ first, second, and third.

His Agony and Our Fellowship

His Destiny
(Matthew 26:36-41, 4:1-4)

Our Destiny as His Disciples
(Matthew 20:22-23; 1 Peter 2:21)

His Dread
(Matthew 26:42-43, 4:5-7)

Our Dread as His Disciples
(Philippians 3:10; John 12:27)

His Devotion
(Matthew 26:44-46, 4:8-11)

Our Devotion as His Disciples
(Luke 12:49; Colossians 1:24)

We can never fathom the agony in Gethsemane, but at least we need not misunderstand it. It is the agony of God and man in one, face-to-face with sin. The agony of our Lord in Gethsemane is not typical of what we go through any more than His cross is typical of our cross. We know nothing about Gethsemane in personal experience. Gethsemane and Calvary stand for something unique; they are the gateway into life for us. We are not dealing here with the typical experience of the saint, but with the way the saintly life has been made possible.

We must read the record of the agony in the light of the temptation three years previously. There are three recorded temptations and three recorded spells of agony in Gethsemane. "Now when the devil had ended every temptation, he departed from Him until an opportune time." In Gethsemane, he came back and was again overthrown. Put away the reverential blasphemy that what Jesus Christ feared in Gethsemane was death on the cross. There was no element of fear in His mind about it; He stated most emphatically that He came on purpose for the cross (Matthew 16:21). His fear in Gethsemane was that He might not get through as Son of Man. Satan's onslaught was that although He would get through as Son of God, it would only be as an isolated figure, and this would mean that He could be no Savior.

Notice again the curious insistence in the records on the fact that our Lord took His disciples with Him, not to share His agony, but to witness it.

His Destiny

> Then Jesus came with them to a place called Gethsemane, and said to the disciples, "Sit here while I go and pray over there" (Matthew 26:36, see also 4:1-4).

At His baptism, the Son of God as the Son of Man, for example, as the whole human race rightly related to God, took on Himself the sin of the whole world: That is why He was baptized with John's baptism, which was a baptism of repentance from sin. It was at His baptism that the Holy

Spirit descended in the form of a dove, and God said, "You are my beloved Son; in you I am well pleased." Before His birth, the angel proclaimed that He should be called Jesus, "for He will save His people from their sins."

This is our Lord's destiny. No human being has a destiny like His, no human being can be a Savior. There is only one Savior, the Lord Jesus Christ, and the profundity of His agony has to do with the fulfilling of His destiny. The only possibility of God being satisfied with the human race is when the whole human race lives as the Son of God lived, and God become incarnate that through His Son every one of us might be enabled to live as He lived.

In God's program, Holy Spirit and man are always identified. Adam was created to be indwelt by Holy Spirit, and God intended him to transform his innocence into holiness by a series of moral choices. But Adam refused to do this; instead, he started up a wrong relationship with the devil, and thereby became the introducer of the heredity of sin into the human race (see Romans 5:12). The entering in of sin meant the departing of the Holy Spirit from the home of man's body, not the departing of him of the Spirit of God as Creator. "Elohim" has reference to God in correspondence with human flesh. When Adam sinned, this correspondence with God ceased until God became manifest in the flesh in Jesus Christ. At His baptism, the Holy Spirit came upon Him as Son of Man, and His coming was the seal of our Lord's accepted vocation. Jesus Christ represented "Elohim," God manifest in the flesh, God and man one in the person of the Son of Man. The sin of the world upon the Son of God rent the Holy Spirit from Him on the cross, and the cry on Calvary is the cry of the Holy Spirit to Jesus Christ: "My God, My God, why have You forsaken me?" It was not the cry of Jesus Christ to His Father. Jesus never spoke to God as "God," He spoke to Him always as "Father." Jesus, knowing that all things were now accomplished ". . . said, 'It is finished.' " These words of our Lord mean that God and the human race in the person of the Son of Man are now one forever in that one person. Holy Spirit may be partaken of by anyone. Anyone can enter into real fellowship with God, into fellowship as real as the communion that Jesus had with His Father, and the way into it is by means of His agony. Ephesians 4:13 is a picture of the human race redeemed by Jesus Christ. He is God's revelation in one person of the human race as God intends it to be.

We are dealing here with revelation, not with experience. Revelation is that upon which we must nourish our faith; experience is that which encourages us that our faith is on the right track. The need to connect revelation and experience must never be overlooked.

In the temptation of our Lord, Satan's first attack was in the physical domain. In Gethsemane, his onslaught is against our Lord as Son of Man, not against Him as Son of God. Satan could not touch Him as Son of God, he could only touch Him as Son of Man; this is his final onslaught on the Son of God as Son of Man. "You will get through as Son of God, I cannot touch You there. But You will never get one member of the human race through with You. Look at Your disciples, they are asleep, they cannot even watch with You. When You come to the cross, Your body will be so tortured and fatigued, so paralyzed with pain, and Your soul will be so darkened and confused, that You will not be able to retain a clear understanding of what You are doing. Your whole personality will be so clouded and crushed by the weight of sin, that You will never get through as man." If Satan had been right, all that would have happened on the cross would have been the death of a martyr; the way into life for us would never have been opened. But if Jesus Christ does get through as Son of Man, it means that the way is open for every one who has been born or ever will be born to get back to God. Satan's challenge to our Lord was that He would not be able to do it; He would only get through as Son of God, because Satan could not touch Him there. The fear that came upon our Lord was that He might die before He reached the cross. He feared that as Son of Man He might die before He had opened the gate for us to get through, and he "was heard because of his godly fear," and was delivered from death in Gethsemane.

When our Lord came to the cross, His body, soul, and spirit were completely triumphant. There was perfect self-possession. Did the pain of the body cloud His mind? "Father, forgive them, for they do not know what they do." His mind was as clear as a sunbeam: "Woman, behold your son!" And He was so triumphant in spirit, in His essential personality, that He cried with a loud voice, "Father, into Your hands I commend My spirit."

Our Destiny as His Disciples

But Jesus answered and said, "You do not know what you ask. Are you able to drink the cup that I am about to drink, and be baptized with the baptism that I am baptized with? They said to Him, "We are able." So He said to them, "You will indeed drink My cup, and be baptized with the baptism that I am baptized with, but to sit on My right hand and on My left is not Mine to give, but it is for those for whom it is prepared by My Father (Matthew 20:22-23; see also 1 Peter 2:21).

Our destiny is determined by our disposition. Our Lord's destiny was determined by His disposition. Our destiny is preordained, but we are free to choose which disposition we will be ruled by. We cannot alter our disposition, but we can choose to let God alter it. If our disposition is to be altered, it must be altered by the Creator, and He will introduce us into a totally new realm by the miracle of His sovereign grace. Redemption means that Jesus Christ can give us a new disposition. At regeneration the Holy Spirit puts in us a totally new disposition, and as we obey that disposition, the life of the Son of God will be manifested in our mortal flesh.

Within certain limits we have the power to choose; for instance, a man has the power to refuse to be born again, but no man has absolute free will. There comes a time when the human will must yield allegiance to a force greater than itself. God is the only being who can act with absolute free will, and when His Spirit comes into us, He makes us free in will; consequently our obedience becomes of value. It is not obedience when one does a thing because he cannot help it, but when a person is made a child of God by redemption, he has the free power to disobey, therefore the power to obey. Our obedience would be of no value at all if the power to sin were taken away.

Our destiny as His disciples is to be in fellowship with God as Jesus was. The cup and the baptism of our Lord are the gateways for every human being to get into perfect oneness with God. Jesus Christ gives us salvation and sanctification, but the places we take hereafter depend upon our obedience and the disposal of the Father. There is no respect of persons with God for salvation, but there are degrees of position thereafter. We are all saved by the cup and the baptism of our Lord, but the position we take individually depends entirely upon our obedience to Him. We are born again through our Lord's cup and baptism, that is, through His fulfilling His destiny; we do not have to agonize and suffer before we can be born from above. All the distress and all the sacrifice in the world will never atone for sin. We must be born again through His sacrifice into the kingdom where He lives, and when we are there, we have to follow in His steps, and we find we can follow now that we have His Spirit, His nature. Our fear starts when we imagine that we have to live this new life by the energy of our human nature, because we know that it cannot be done, and every time we think of what we were before, we falter. The Bible reveals that when the Holy Spirit has come into us, every command of God is an enabling. Jesus Christ gives the power of His own disposition to anyone, that is why He is apparently so merciless on those of us who have received the Holy Spirit, because His demands on us are made according to His disposition, and not according to our human nature. The old nature says it cannot be done. Jesus Christ says it can be done: "I did it, and I can do it in you if you will enter my life by means of my death." It is no use trying to be what we are not. We are children of God when we are born from above, and God will never shield us from the requirements of being His children. "Follow His steps"—that is the conduct of regenerate human nature.

The life of Jesus is the life of the normal man of God, but we cannot begin to live it unless we are born from above. Unless we have been taken up into His destiny, we cannot fulfill our own destiny. If we are born from above, are we trying to follow His steps, trying to work out in our mortal flesh that which God has worked in (Philippians 2:12-13)?

Salvation is a sovereign gift of the redemption of the

Lord Jesus. Many will be saved through the fulfilling of the destiny of the Son of Man who have not been worth anything to God in this life: Their lives have been self-centered and wrong, they have not been lived on the foundation of the Son of God. Our destiny is to work out what God works in. It is not that our eternal salvation depends upon our doing it, but our value to God does, and also our position in the kingdom of God.

His Dread

He went away again a second time and prayed, saying, "O My Father, if this cup cannot pass away from Me, unless I drink it, Your will be done" (Matthew 26:42-43, see also 4:5-7).

The disciples are the representatives of the human race in connection with redemption, and Satan's sneer in Gethsemane is, "You will never do it. These men are the specimens of the best You have, and they are asleep. You should have gone to heaven from the Mount of Transfiguration, but instead, You came down and declared You would redeem the human race, and I am determined that You will not." Our Lord's dread in Gethsemane was born of the knowledge that if He did not get through as Son of Man, the redemption of mankind was hopeless; we could only then have imitated Him, we could never have known Him as Savior.

This is the agony of God as Man, not a human agony. Our Lord did not want human sympathy, His agony was infinitely profounder than human sympathy could come anywhere near. The darkness was produced because it looked as if Satan were going to triumph, and the disciples, who represented the new humanity, were without the slightest element of understanding what Jesus Christ was doing. He "offered up prayers and supplications with vehement cries and tears to Him who was able to save Him from death, and was heard because of His godly fear." His prayer was answered every time, and when He came to the cross His relationship to His mother, and to John, and to His murderers showed that His mind and His reason were triumphantly clear. It was not only a sign that our Lord had triumphed, but that He had triumphed to save the human race, so that every human being can get through into the presence of God because of all the Son of Man went through. Jesus Christ is either all that the New Testament claims Him to be—the Redeemer of the human race—or else a futile dreamer, and the only proof is in personal experience. Can God form the life that His Son lived in us? Jesus Christ claims that He can. Then have we let Him do it?

Our Dread as His Disciples

> That I may know Him and the power of His resurrection, and the fellowship of His sufferings, being conformed to His death (Philippians 3:10; see also John 12:27).

Our dread as His disciples is lest we fail Jesus Christ in our service, lest in our experience of the revelation we forget the God who gave us the experience, forget all about Jesus Christ. As disciples we have not to serve God in our own way, not to tell Him what we are going to do for Him, not to ask Him to baptize us with the Holy Spirit to make us something. "If you would be my disciple," says Jesus, "give up your right to yourself to me, and take up your cross daily." No one can carry the cross of God. The cross of God is the redemption of the world. The cross we have to carry is that we have deliberately given up our right to ourselves to Jesus Christ, and we steadily refuse to be appealed to on any other line than He was appealed to when He was here. With regard to all the pleasures and sciences and interests of this life, ask this simple consideration, "Is this the kind of thing the Son of God is doing in the world, or is it what the prince of this world is doing?" Not, "Is it right?" but "Is it the kind of thing the Son of God would be doing in the world?" If it is not, then don't touch it. If you only give up wrong things for Jesus Christ, don't talk any more about being in love with Him. If you want to do a thing all the time, it is no virtue not to do it! Jesus Christ takes the "want to" out of us and enables us to do in this world the things He would be doing if He were here. We say, "Why shouldn't I? It isn't wrong!" What a sordid thing to say! When we love a person, do we only give up what is wrong for him? Love is not measured by what it gets, but by what it costs. And our relationship to Jesus Christ can never be on the line of "Why shouldn't I do this?" Our Lord simply says, "If any man will be my disciple, those are the conditions" (see Luke 14:26-27, 33). Is He worth it? Will He cast it up at us that we never gave up anything for Him? No, He will never do that, He will never tell us what sneaks we have been, but we will find it out (see Matthew 10:26). Our dread is to be—lest we forget Him. Do we know Jesus Christ better today than ever before?

If we have been put right with God through the agony of the Son of God, have we enthroned Him as Lord and Master as well? (see John 13:13, Luke 6:46). Is He absolute master of our body? (see 1 Corinthians 3:16-17). We have no business to be master of our own body. Our dread is lest we forget that our body is the temple of the Holy Spirit. We are to know Jesus Christ and the power of His resurrection in our body, to know the fellowship of His sufferings in our body. "If anyone desires to come after Me, let him deny himself." There is no "if" in connection with salvation, only in connection with discipleship. The conditions of discipleship are found in Luke 14:26-27, 33. If the commands of Jesus Christ in our life clash with the most sacred relationships on earth, it must be instant obedience to Him. We must hate the claim that contends with His claim; hate it, that is, in comparison with our love to Him. We must abandon to God at all costs. Abandon is of infinitely more value than self-scrutiny.

His Devotion

> So He left them, went away again, and prayed the third time, saying the same words. Then He came to His disciples and said to them, "Are you still sleeping and resting? Behold, the hour is at hand, and the Son of Man is being betrayed into the hands of sinners. Rise, let us be going. See, He who betrays Me is at hand" (Matthew 26:44-46, 4:8-11).

"Still sleeping? It is all right now, it is all finished; the Son of Man is betrayed into the hands of sinners." That is a joyful utterance. Our Lord is absolutely sure that as a representative of man before God He will get the whole human race through, in spite of everything the devil can do, and the cross is an absolute triumph. Our Lord, as Son of Man, has been through the depths of His agony in Gethsemane, and He has won at every point. He has won for the minds and souls and spirits of men. Everything that makes up a human personality is redeemed absolutely, and no matter whether a person be a vile sinner or as clean as the rich young ruler, he can enter into the marvelous life with God through the way made by the Son of Man.

"Father, into Your hands I commend My spirit," that is, the spirit of the Son of Man, the spirit of the whole human race represented by the Son of Man getting through to God on the cross. "Though He was a Son, yet He learned obedience by the things which He suffered" (Hebrews 5:8). He did not learn to be a son, He was a Son, and He came to redeem as Man, and He learned obedience as a Redeemer by suffering. His agony is the basis of the simplicity of our salvation. His suffering is the basis of all our light and liberty and joy. His cross makes it simple enough for anyone to get into the presence of God.

Our Lord in His agony was devoted to God's purpose. The supreme obedience of Jesus was never to the needs of people, but always to the will of His Father. The church goes astray whenever she makes the need the call. Then need is never the call, the need is the opportunity; the call is the call of God.

Our Devotion as His Disciples

I came to send fire on the earth, and how I wish it were already kindled! (Luke 12:49; see also Colossians 1:24).

"Our God is a consuming fire," and when God comes on to this earth in the effective working of the redemption of Jesus Christ, He brings pain and havoc and disaster (see Matthew 10:34). The first result of the redemption of Jesus Christ in human life is havoc. If any human life can stand before God on its own basis, Calvary is much ado about nothing. If it can be proved that rationalism is the basis of human life, then the New Testament is nonsense; instead of its being a revelation, it is a cunningly devised fable. There is no need for redemption; Jesus Christ is nothing but a martyr, of whom it was true that He was stricken, smitten of God and afflicted. If we can stand before God apart from Jesus Christ, we have proved that Calvary is not needed. As soon as Jesus Christ comes in, He produces havoc because the whole world system is arrayed against His redemption. It was the world system of His day, and particularly the religious system, that killed the Son of God.

"And fill up in my flesh what is lacking in the afflictions of Christ"—for redemption's sake? No, "for the sake of His body, which is the church." On the ground of Jesus Christ's redemption, we can enter into identification with His sufferings, but we do not need to unless we like. First Corinthians 13 and Matthew 4:43-48 are practical homecoming Christian truths. "Come to Me . . . . Take My yoke upon you, and learn from Me," "then go and bear with others for my sake." What have we suffered for Jesus Christ? Think of the passionate indignation we get into when someone slanders us! "Consider him." We do not need to take the blow, but if we do not, it will go back on Him. We will get off scot-free, and everyone will applaud us for doing so, but the blow will fall upon Jesus Christ. If we let it come on us, it will not fall on Him. We have always the privilege of going the second mile. It is never our duty to do it, but will we go the second mile with God? Are we deliberately filling up that which remains behind of His sufferings or becoming mere critical centers? If we have been brought into a right relationship with God by the redemption of Jesus Christ, He expects us to put on His yoke and to learn of Him.

The devotion of the saint is to "fill up that which is

behind the afflictions of Christ for his body's sake," nothing remains behind to be filled up for redemption's sake. How did Jesus Christ suffer? Because people misunderstood Him? Because He was persecuted? Because He could not get on with me? No, He suffered for one thing only—that men might be saved; He let almighty God do His whole will in and through Him without asking His permission. He suffered "according to the will of God."

How can we fill up the sufferings that remain behind? First John 5:16 is an indication of one way, that of intercession. Remember, no one has time to pray, he has to take time from other things that are valuable to understand how necessary time for prayer is. The things that act like thorns and stings in our personal lives will go away when we pray; we won't feel the smart any more, because we have got God's point of view about them. Prayer means that we get into union with God's view of other people. Our devotion as saints is to identify ourselves with God's interests in other lives. God pays no attention to our personal affinities; He expects us to identify ourselves with His interests in others.

His Cross and Our Discipleship

The Collision of God and Sin (Acts 2:36)
The Sacrifice to Christ of Myself
(Romans 12:1-2; Matthew 16:24; Luke 9:23)

The Contradiction of God and Satan
(John 12:31-33)
The Suffering for Christ of Myself
(Colossians 1:24; 2 Corinthians 1:5; Philippians 3:10)

The Center of God and Salvation
(2 Corinthians 5:14)
The Sacrament of God in Myself
(Acts 20:24; 1 Corinthians 15:30)

There is a difference between revelation and experience. As Christians we must have an experience, but we must believe a great deal more than we can experience.

For instance, no Christian can experience the cross of Christ, but he can experience God becoming incarnate and he can experience the incoming of the life of God by regeneration. No Christian can experience the personal advent of the Holy Spirit onto this earth, but he can experience the indwelling of the Holy Spirit. A New Testament Christian is one who bases all his thinking on these revelations. He experiences the regenerating power of God, and then goes on to build up his mind in the most holy faith. Until a man is born again, he cannot think as a Christian. Belief of doctrine does not make a man a Christian. There are those who emphasize doctrine, they would go to martyrdom for the faith; while others emphasize experience and take everything revealed in the Bible as picturing our experience. Either of these views is likely to become a dangerous side track.

Jesus Christ took thirty-three years over the historic completion of redemption to exhibit what God's normal man was like. He lived the pattern normal life of a man as God wants it to be, and He demands of us that we live as He did. But how are we to begin to do it? We did not come into the world as God Incarnate came. He came from preexisting deity; we are born with the heredity of sin. How are we to enter into the life He lived? By His cross and by no other way. We do not enter into the life of God by imitation, or by vows, or by ceremonies, or by church membership; we enter into it by its entering into us at regeneration. The cross of Jesus Christ is the gateway into His life.

The cross is not the cross of a man but the cross of God, and the cross of God can never be realized in human experience. Beware of saying that Jesus Christ was a martyr. Today He is frequently looked upon as a martyr: His life is acknowledged to be very beautiful, but the atonement and the cross are not being given their rightful place, and the Bible is being robbed of its magnitude and virility. The death of our Lord was not the death of a martyr but the exhibition of the heart of God, and the gateway whereby any member of the human race can enter into union with God. The cross is the center of time and of eternity, the answer to the enigmas of both.

The Collision of God and Sin

Therefore let all the house of Israel know assuredly that God has made this Jesus, whom you crucified, both Lord and Christ (Acts 2:36).

The cross of Jesus is the revelation of God's judgment of sin. It is not the cross of a martyr; it is the substitution of Jesus for sinful humanity. The cross did not happen to Jesus; He came on purpose for it. The whole purpose of the incarnation is the cross: "The Lamb slain from the foundation of the world." The cross is beyond time; the actual crucifixion is the historical revelation of the heart nature of the Trinity of God. The symbolic figure of the nature of God is not a circle, complete and self-centered; God is not all. The symbol of God's nature is the cross, whose arms stretch out to limitless reaches.

The cross of Jesus Christ is a revelation; our cross is an experience. If we neglect for one moment the basal revelation of the cross, we will make shipwreck of our faith, no matter what our experience is. The test of our spiritual life is our understanding of the cross. The cross of Jesus is often wrongly taken as a type of the cross we have to carry. Jesus did not say, "If any one will come after Me, let him take up My cross," but "let him deny himself, and take up His cross, and follow Me." Our cross becomes our divinely appointed privilege by means of His cross. We are never called upon to carry his cross. We have so hallowed the cross by twenty centuries of emotion and sentiment that it sounds a very beautiful and pathetic thing to talk about carrying our cross. But a wooden cross with iron nails in it is a clumsy thing to carry. The real cross was like that, and do we imagine that the external cross was more ugly than our actual one? Or that the thing that tore our Lord's hands and feet was not really so terrible as our imagination of it?

Do we agree with God's judgment upon sin in the cross? There is a difference between sin and sins. Sin is a heredity; sins are acts for which we are responsible. Sin is a thing we are born with and we cannot touch it. God touches sin in redemption, and the cross reveals the clash of God and sin. If we do not put to death the things in us that are not of God, they will put to death the things that are of God. There is never any alternative, some thing must die in us—either sin or the life of God. If we agree theologically with God's condemnation of sin on the cross, then what about sin in our own heart? Do we agree with God's verdict on sin and lust in our lives? The moment we do agree, we may be delivered from it. It is a question of agreeing with God's verdict on sin and of will. Will we go through the condemnation now? If we will, there is no more condemnation for us, and the salvation of Jesus Christ is made actual in our lives. Unless our salvation works out through our fingertips and everywhere else, there is nothing to it; it is religious humbug.

The Sacrifice to Christ of Myself. "I beseech you therefore, brethren, by the mercies of God, that you present your bodies a living sacrifice, holy, acceptable to God, which is your reasonable service. And do not be conformed to this world, but be transformed by the renewing of your mind, that you may prove what is that good and acceptable and perfect will of God" (Romans 12:1-2; see also Matthew 16:24; Luke 9:23).

"Present your bodies a living sacrifice." We cannot present an unholy thing at the altar, and Paul's word "brethren" means saints. It is only from the standpoint of sanctification that these verses apply. Our Lord says to those who have entered into His life by means of His Cross: "Let him deny himself, and take up his cross, and follow Me," not "Let him give up sin." Any man will give up sinning if he knows how to, but "Let him deny himself," that is, "give up his right to himself to me." Our cross is what we hold before the world—the fact that we are sanctified to do nothing but God's will. We have given away our right to ourselves forever, and the cross we take up is a sign in heaven, on earth, and to hell that we are His, and no longer our own. The right to ourselves is the only thing we have to give to God. We cannot give our natural possessions, because they have been given to us. If we had not our right to ourselves by God's creation of us, we should have nothing to give and consequently could not be held responsible.

Jesus Christ is not dealing with sin here (sin is dealt with by His cross), but with what has been referred to as the natural life, the life symbolized by Mary, the mother of Jesus, that must be sacrificed not annihilated. The idea of sacrifice is giving back to God the best we have so that He may make it His and ours forever. Have we done it? Have we as saints given up our right to ourselves to Him? Or do we while accepting His salvation thoroughly object to giving up our right to ourselves to Him? Sanctification has to do with separating the holy life to God's uses. "And for their sakes I sanctify Myself, that they also may be sanctified by the truth" (John 17:19).

We are apt to imagine that the cross we have to carry means the ordinary troubles and trials of life, but we must have these whether we are Christians or not. Neither is our cross-suffering for conscience' sake. Our cross is something that comes only with the peculiar relationship of a disciple to Jesus Christ; it is the evidence that we have denied our right to ourselves. "I have been crucified with Christ; it is no longer I who live, but Christ lives in me . . ." (Galatians 2:20). It is not only that we give up our right to ourselves to Jesus Christ, but that determinedly we relate ourselves to life so that we may be appealed to only by the things that appeal to Him and do in the world only the things with which He is associated. There are myriad right things in this world that our Lord would not touch, relationships that He described by the "eye," and the "right arm." Our right arm is not a bad thing; it is one of the best things we have. But Jesus said, "If it offends you in your walk with me, cut it off." Most of us balk at this: We do not object to being delivered from sin, but we do not intend to give up the right to ourselves to Him. The only right a Christian has is the right to give up his rights. Unless we are willing to give up good things for Jesus Christ, we have no realization of who He is. "But really I cannot give up things that are quite legitimate!" Then never mention the word love again in connection with Jesus Christ if you cannot give up the best you have for Him. This is the essential nature of love in the natural life; otherwise, it is a farce to call it love, it is not love, but lust. When we come to our relationship with Jesus Christ, this is the love He demands of us. If we have entered into the experience of regeneration through His Cross, these are the conditions of discipleship (see Luke 14:26-27, 33). Always notice the "if" in connection with discipleship, there is never any compulsion. "If anyone comes to me, and does not hate . . . , he cannot be my disciple." He may be anything else—a very fascinating person, a most delightful asset to modern civilization—but Jesus Christ says, "he cannot be my disciple." A man may be saved without being a disciple, and it is the point of discipleship that is always kicked against. Our Lord is not talking of eternal salvation but of the possibility of our being of temporal worth to Himself.

How many of us are of any worth to Jesus Christ? Our attitude is rather that we are much obliged to God for saving us, but the idea of giving up our chances to realize ourselves in life is too extravagantly extreme. Some of us will take all God has to give us while we take good care not to give Him anything back.

The sacrifice of myself to Christ is not a revelation, but an experience. Have I sacrificed myself to Him, or have I refused to give up my right to myself to Him because there are several things I want to do? "There are so many other interests in my life, and, of course, God will not expect it of me." Always state things to yourself to realize whether you ruggedly are what you sentimentally think you ought to be, and you will soon know the kind of humbug you are. Spiritual reality is what is wanted. "I surrender all"—and you feel as if you did. That is the awkward thing. The point is whether, as God engineers your circumstances, you find that you really have surrendered. As soon as you do surrender, you are made so much one with your Lord that the thought of what it cost never enters anymore.

The Contradiction of God and Satan

"Now is the judgment of this world; now the ruler of this world will be cast out. And I, if I am lifted up from the earth, will draw all peoples to Myself." This He said, signifying by what death He would die (John 12:31-33).

The prince of this world and Satan are synonymous terms. Satan, or the Devil, is the manifestation of the evil in which man became involved in the communication set-up between them (see Genesis 3). Our Lord, in saying to Peter,

"Get behind Me, Satan," then defined Satan: "You are not mindful of the things of God, but the things of men." What was it that Peter was mindful of? Self-pity. "Pity Yourself, Lord: this will not be to You." And Jesus "turned and said to Peter, 'Get behind me, Satan! You are an offense to Me.' " Peter's appeal was made on the ground of self-interest, and the prince of this world governs everything on that basis. Self-realization is the essential principle of his government. "Whoever therefore will be a friend of the world is the enemy of God." The world is that system of things that organizes its life without any thought of Jesus Christ. Paul says that the lost are those whose minds are blinded by the god of this world (see 2 Corinthians 4:3, 4). Nothing blinds the mind to the claims of Jesus Christ more effectively than a good, clean-living, upright life based on self-realization. For a thing to be satanic does not mean that it is abominable and immoral. The satanically managed person is moral, upright, proud, and individual; he is absolutely self-governed and has no need of God. The prince of this world is judged forever at the cross. If we enter into the kingdom of God through the cross of Christ, self-realization cannot get through with us, it must be left outside. The cross of Christ reveals the contradiction of God and Satan. The disposition of self-realization is the manifestation in us of the devil as Satan, and when we come to the cross, we leave Satan outside. Satan cannot take one step inside the cross.

The Sufferings for Christ of Myself. "I now rejoice in my sufferings for you, and fill up in my flesh what is lacking in the afflictions of Christ, for the sake of His body, which is the church" (Colossians 1:24; see also 2 Corinthians 1:5; Philippians 3:10). That is suffering without any notice from the world except its ridicule. It is not suffering like Christ, it is suffering for Christ. It is not suffering for the sake of redemption; we have nothing to do with redemption, that is completed. We have to fill up "what is lacking in the afflictions of Christ for the sake of His body, which is the church."

When by the cross of Christ we have entered into the experience of identification with our Lord, then there comes the practical working out of Matthew 11:29: "Take my yoke upon you, and learn from Me, for I am gentle and lowly in heart." When we learn of Jesus, we will not grouse at a dispensation of God's providence that we cannot understand; we shall not give way to self-pity and say, "Why should this happen to me?" Jesus said, "Let him . . . take up his cross, and follow Me." This means putting into exercise 1 Corinthians 13 and deliberately identifying ourselves with God's interests in others, and it involves a moral decision on our part. God will bring across our path people who embody the characteristics that we have shown to Him: stubbornness, pride, conceit, opinionatedness, sensuality, a hundred little meannesses. "Now," He says, "love them as I have loved you." It works in this way: We see that someone is going to get the better of us, and every logical power in us says, "Resent it." Morally speaking, we should. But Jesus Christ says, "When you are insulted, not only do not resent it, but exhibit the Son of God." The disciple realizes that his Lord's honor is at stake in his life, not his own honor. A coward does not hit back because he is afraid; a strong man refuses to hit back because he is strong. But in appearance they are both the same, and that is where the intense humiliation of being a Christian comes in. The Lord is asking us to go the second mile with Him, and if we take the blow, we will save Him. We can always avoid letting Jesus Christ get the blow by taking it ourselves. Be absolutely abandoned to God, it is only your own reputation that is at stake. People will not discredit God; they will only think you are a fool.

After the resurrection, Jesus Christ did not invite the disciples to a time of communion on the Mount of Transfiguration, He said—"Feed My sheep." When God gives a person work to do, it is seldom work that seems at all appropriate to his natural ability. Paul, lion-hearted genius though he was, spent his time teaching the most ignorant people. The evidence that we are in love with God is that we identify ourselves with His interests in others, and other people are the exact expression of what we ourselves are. That is the humiliating thing! Jesus Christ came down to a most miserably insignificant people to redeem them. When He has lifted us into relationship with Himself, He expects us to identify ourselves with His interests in others.

The Center of God and Salvation

> For the love of Christ constrains us, because we judge thus: that if One died for all, then all died (2 Corinthians 5:14).

We cannot be saved by consecration, or by praying, or by giving ourselves up to God. We can only be saved by the cross of Jesus Christ. Salvation is an absolutely free, unmerited gift of God. We would a hundred times rather that God told us to do something than we would accept His salvation as a gift. The center of salvation is the cross of Jesus Christ. And why it is so easy to obtain salvation is because it cost God so much. And why it is so difficult to experience salvation is because human conceit will not accept, nor believe, nor have anything to do with unmerited salvation.

We have not to experience God saving the world; it is a revelation that God has saved the world through Christ, and we can enter into the experience of His salvation through the cross. The cross is the point where God and sinful man merge with a crash, and the way to life is opened, but the crash is on the heart of God. God is always the sufferer.

The Sacrament of God in Myself. "But none of these things move me; nor do I count my life dear to myself, so that I may finish my race with joy, and the ministry which I received from the Lord Jesus, to testify to the gospel of the grace of God" (Acts 20:24; see also 1 Corinthians 15:30).

"Nor do I count my life dear to myself." Paul was absolutely indifferent to any other consideration than that of fulfilling the ministry he had received. He could never be appealed to by those who urged him to remain in a certain place because he was being of so much use there. Watch our Lord also. He went through villages and cities where He was marvelously used, but the great characteristic of His earthly life was that He steadfastly set His face to go to Jerusalem; He never stayed in a place because He had been of use there (Mark 1:37-38). Beware of the sweet sisters and beloved brothers who say to you, "Now do consider whether you will not be of more use here than anywhere else." Probably you will, and in the passing of the months, you will become moldy bread instead of eating bread. We have nothing to do with God's purpose but only with the sacrament of God in us, that is, the real presence of God coming through the common elements of our lives (see John 7:37-39). The measure of our service for God is not our usefulness to others. We have nothing to do with the estimate of others, nor with success in service; we have to see that we fulfill our ministry. "As You sent Me into the world, I also have sent them into the world" (John 17:18). Our Lord's first obedience was not to the needs of people, not to the consideration of where He was most useful, but to the will of His Father, and the first need of our life is not to be useful to God, but to do God's will. How are we to know the will of God? By living in Romans 12:1-2. By being renewed in the spirit of the mind and refusing to be conformed to this age, we shall make out "what is that good and acceptable and perfect will of God."

It Is Finished
John 19:30

The transfiguration, as we have already seen, was the Great Divide in the life of our Lord. He stood in the perfect, spotless holiness of His manhood; then He turned His back on the glory and came down from the Mount to be identified with sin, that through His death fallen humanity might not only be redeemed, but enabled to have a conscious entrance into the life He lived.

The church of God is in danger of forgetting what Jesus Christ came for, and presenting Him as a mere example. When the conscience of the church is awakened and made to face the cross of Christ, and to take our Lord at His own estimate of Himself, she will realize the meaning of Paul's words: "For I have determined not to know anything among you, except Jesus Christ . . . ." And Him risen? And Him glorified? No. " . . . and him crucified." The resurrection and glorification through the ascension are understandable only by the cross. The death of Jesus Christ holds the secret of the mind of God.

The Vicarious Visitation of God

The next day John saw Jesus coming toward him, and said, "Behold! the Lamb of God who takes away the sin of the world!" (John 1:29).

148

At the outset of our Lord's public ministry He accepted His vocation, which was to "bear away the sin of the world." We must never forget that. John's baptism was a baptism of repentance for the remission of sins, and that was the baptism with which Jesus was baptized. "Permit it to be so now, for thus it is fitting for us to fulfill all righteousness"; and right through to the end, our Lord was identified with that one thing—that is, sin.

The agony in Gethsemane reveals the last reach of the unfathomable depths to which our Lord went in that identification. "Christ has redeemed us from the curse of the law, having become a curse for us." "Behold! the Lamb of God, who takes away the sin of the world!" These were almost the first words John the Baptist spoke about Jesus. And almost the last words Jesus spoke were to a criminal: "Today you will be with Me in paradise." The last possible reach of faith is the cry of a sinner who begins to realize that God can save him. As soon as he cries out to God he will find the marvel of Jesus Christ's salvation wrought in his personal experience.

The death of Jesus Christ was not the death of a martyr; it was the death of God (see Acts 20:28). The Son of God was put to death by humanity based on self-realization. Through the redemption, self-realization is turned into Christ-realization—that is, a man enters into a relationship that puts to death not the Son of God, but the disposition of sin. The essence of sin is my claim to my right to myself.

The Vanishing Vision of God

My God, my God, why have You forsaken Me? (Matthew 27:46).

This is a cry from the depths; it is unfathomable. It is recorded by the Spirit of God, and we are meant to look into all that is recorded. God has nothing to conceal in His great purpose for the salvation of man, and we are meant to look into the depths that this cry represents.

Who is it that experiences God-forsakenness? Is it the lonely missionary with no comradeship? He is the one who knows the nearness of God. The ones who understand the experience of God-forsakenness are men like Cain: "My punishment is greater than I can bear" (Genesis 4:13); men like Esau: ". . . an exceeding great and bitter cry"; men like Saul: "God has departed from me and does not answer me any more."

If our Lord had never known the "vanishing vision of God," He could not have been a complete Savior. Agony that has God behind it can be turned into triumph; but think of agony in which there is no God, neither in heaven above nor earth beneath, only the terror of an accusing conscience. No human sympathy can touch that desolation. In all probability the person is to blame for it, and just because he is, no human sympathy can reach him. Anyone can have a fellow feeling for a poor, unfortunate being and can sympathize with him, but who among us can understand agony that goes deeper down than can be put into words? Who but Jesus Christ?

"Without holiness, no man shall see the Lord." God cannot look on sin; and on the cross, the world's sin and the world's punishment met in the Person of the Son of Man. The cross of Christ means that the salvation of God goes deeper down than the deepest depths of iniquity man can commit. No person can get beyond the reach of Jesus; He made a way back to the throne of God from the very heart of hell by His tremendous atonement.

There is a conception abroad today that the incarnation is something altogether apart from the idea of atonement. According to the Bible, the Son of God became incarnate in order to bear away the sin of the human race. Before one can take upon himself the sin of a family, he must be a member of it. Jesus Christ took upon Himself the form of the human family that was cursed with sin, and in that human form He lived a spotlessly holy life; and by means of His death He can introduce the shamed members of the human family into the life He lived.

Our Lord made human solidarity His own: He represents the vilest sinner out of hell and the purest saint out of heaven. He stands as the one great representative of the human race, atoning for its sin. It beggars language to describe what He did: He went into identification with the depths of damnation, that the human race might be delivered. "When you make his soul an offering for sin . . ." We praise God for our salvation, but have we ever once thought how it came to us? Through the deep shadows, deeper than any human mind can ever go.

Again, beware of saying that Jesus Christ took on Himself the sin of the world by sympathy; that would mean that we can take on His righteousness only by sympathy. Jesus Christ took on the sin of the world by being identified with it. "But of him are you in Christ Jesus, who was made for us . . . righteousness."

The Victorious Voice for God

And when Jesus had cried with a loud voice, He said, "Father, into Your hands I commend My spirit" (Luke 23:46).

The cross is a tragedy to man, but a tremendous triumph to God, an absolute triumph. Listen to the clear, ringing voice: "Father, into Your hands I commend My spirit!" The spirit of the Son of God only? No, the spirit of the whole human race incarnated in the Savior of the world. My spirit was there, your spirit was there, and by God's mighty grace and the gift of His Spirit given by our Lord after He ascended, we can know experientially His complete salvation for body, soul, and spirit.

Never consider this passage in a shallow way—that on the cross the physical sufferings of Jesus were so great that His mind was blinded and He imagined His Father had gone from Him. That understanding does not touch the depths of identification with sin to which our Lord went. Neither is it true to say that God was angry and hid His face from Him. If one may put it so, God was never more pleased with His Son than when He bridged the gulf between God and man by the sacrifice of Himself.

When the New Testament speaks of the sufferings of Christ, it is suffering in connection with our salvation and in no other connection: "Ought not the Christ to have suffered these things and to enter into His glory?" He suffered "according to the will of God." It is not the suffering of a human being; this is the eternal Christ of God "tasting death for every man." The agony in Gethsemane represents the incomprehensible mystery of 2 Corinthians 5:21. "For He has made Him . . . to be sin for us . . ."

It is only by thinking along these lines, bare-souled and humbled before God, that we can understand what a wonderful thing our salvation is. Salvation is an immense marvel to me—that I, a sinner, can be made into a saint—but it is possible only because of what Jesus Christ did. Are the unfathomable depths of suffering through which our Lord went to mean less than entire deliverance from sin for us? The reason sanctification is so easy for us is because of Gethsemane. The Holy Spirit, received as a gift into our personal life, brings the supernatural marvel of the salvation wrought by our Lord. That is the message the Spirit of God has given to be proclaimed to the world. It matters not how sin-stained a person may be—through the death of Jesus Christ on the cross, he can partake of that wondrous salvation.

"I have finished the work which You have given Me to do." What was finished? The rehabilitation of the human race back to where God designed it to be. It was not the salvation of individual men and women like you and me that was being finished; but the whole human race was put on the basis of redemption. Redemption is not going to be finished; it is finished. Believing does not make a man redeemed; believing enables him to realize that he is redeemed. To any man who thinks, the basis of life is not reason, but redemption. The miracle of the work of God is performed when he places himself on the "It is finished" side of the cross.

We take our salvation and our sanctification much too cheaply. We ought to rejoice when a person says he is saved, but remember what it cost God to make His grace a free gift. It cost agony that we cannot begin to understand. The Christian faith means that the historic cross of Christ is the pinhole in actual history through which we get a view of the purpose of God all through. Jesus Christ is "the Lamb slain from the foundation of the world."

His Resurrection and Our Life

His Resurrection Declared (Mark 16:5-8)

Our Eternal Life (John 20:22)

His Resurrection Destiny (Luke 24:26)

Our Experimental Life
(Philippians 3:10; Romans 6:23)

His Resurrection Deity (John 20:17)

Our Entire Life (Colossians 3:1-4)

We must always distinguish between the truths we receive as revelations and what we experience of God's grace. We experience the wonderful reality of God's salvation and sanctification in our actual lives, but we have also to receive into our minds and souls divine revelations that we cannot experience. We cannot experience Jesus Christ rising from the dead; we cannot experience His destiny or His deity, but we must understand where the regenerating forces in our lives come from. The New Testament insists on an instructed mind as well as a vital experience.

His Resurrection Declared

And entering the tomb, they saw a young man
clothed in a long white robe sitting on the right side;
and they were alarmed. But he said to them, "Do not
be alarmed. You seek Jesus of Nazareth, who was
crucified. He is risen! He is not here. See the place
where they laid him (Mark 16:5-8).

Our Lord died and was buried and He rose again, and this
is the declaration of the resurrection in all its incredibleness.
Any question that arises in connection with the resurrection
arises in the minds of those who do not accept the necessity
of being born from above. There is always a quarrel between
our common sense and the revelations made in God's Book.
We must lose our soul to find it. We have to be born from
above and receive Holy Spirit into our spirit, and then begin
to construct another soul, or way of reasoning, and to do this
we must accept not only the facts that come to us through
our common sense, but the facts that come by revelation. We
say "Seeing is believing," but it is not. We must believe a
thing is possible before we should believe it even though we
saw it (see John 20:29).

Our Eternal Life

"And when He had said this, He breathed on them , and
said to them, 'Receive the Holy Spirit' " (John 20:22).
Eternal life is the gift of the Lord Jesus Christ. "He who
believes in Me has everlasting life" (John 6:47); that is, the
life He manifested in His human flesh when He was here.
And says Jesus, ". . . you have no life in you" (John 6:53). His
life is not ours by natural birth, and it can only be given to

us by means of His cross. Our Lord's cross is the gateway into His life; His resurrection means that He has power now to convey that life to us (see John 17:2).

The onslaught of Satan in Gethsemane was that Jesus Christ would never get through His agony as Son of Man. As Son of God, Satan could not prevent His getting through, but his challenge was that he would prevent Jesus Christ bringing one soul through with Him—Satan was hopelessly defeated. By the death of the Son of Man upon the cross, the door is opened for any individual to go straight into the presence of God, and by the resurrection our Lord can impart to us His own life. When we are born from above, we receive from the risen Lord His very life; our human spirit is quickened by the incoming of the life of God. That is the marvel of the power of the Lord Jesus Christ through His resurrection. "I would know Him in the power of His resurrection" (Philippians 3:10, Moffatt).

Holy Spirit, salvation, and eternal life are inter-changeable terms. "Holy Spirit" is the experiential name for eternal life working in human beings here and now. The only thing that makes eternal life actual is the entrance of the Holy Spirit by commitment to Jesus Christ. Our beliefs will mock us unless something comes into us from God, because nothing has any power to alter us except the incoming of the life of God. The Holy Spirit is the One who makes experientially real in us what Jesus Christ did for us. The Holy Spirit is the deity in proceeding power who applies the atonement to our experience. Jesus Christ came to redeem us, to put us right with God, to deliver us from the power of death, to reveal God the Father. When we receive the Holy Spirit, He will make experientially real in us all that Jesus Christ came to do. The great need for men and women is to receive the Holy Spirit. Our creeds teach us to believe in the Holy Spirit; the New Testament says we must receive Him (see Luke 11:13). Are you powerless in your life? Then get at reality! Ask God for the Holy Spirit; that is, His eternal life, and you will begin to manifest in your mortal flesh the life of Jesus. One day we shall have a body like His body, but we can know now the efficacy of our Lord's resurrection. We can receive the Holy Spirit and experientially know His salvation.

His Resurrection Destiny

> Ought not the Christ to have suffered these things
> and to enter into His glory? (Luke 24:26).

The sufferings of Jesus Christ were not an accident, they were what He came for; He knew that His life was to be a ransom for many. Those who do not suffer in this world are not worth their salt. The finest men and women suffer, and the devil uses their sufferings to slander God. God is after one thing—bringing many sons to glory—and He does not care what it costs us any more than He cared what it cost Him. God has taken the responsibility for the possibility of sin, and the proof that He did so is the cross. He is the suffering God, not One who reigns above in calm disdain. "Though He was a Son, yet He learned obedience by the things which He suffered." He did not learn to be a Son, but because He was a Son, He deliberately chose to obey God through suffering. His resurrection destiny is to suffer and to enter into glory so that He may bring "many sons to glory." We must beware lest we put the emphasis of strain and suffering on the wrong thing. Salvation and eternal life are easy for us to obtain because of what they cost God. If we find it difficult to come to God, it is because we will try to drag our human pride through. If we will only come with the simplicity of a child, there is no need for any agony at all. We can receive the marvelous revelation of salvation and experience the impartation of the life of the risen Lord Jesus, but self-realization and self-interest and sin must all be renounced. Never sympathize with a soul who finds it difficult to get through to God. It is perilously easy to sympathize with Satan, instead of with God (see Matthew 16:23). No one can be more tender to men and women than God. We are slandering God if we sympathize with the willfulness of a person and think how difficult God makes it for him. It is never hard to get to God unless our willfulness makes it hard.

Our Lord rose to an absolutely new life, to a life He did not live before He was incarnate; He rose to a life that had never been before. There had been resurrections before the resurrection of Jesus Christ, but they were all resuscitations to the same kind of life as heretofore. Jesus Christ rose to a totally new life and to a totally different relationship to men and women. The resurrection of Jesus Christ grants Him the right to give His own destiny to any human being; that is, to make us the sons and daughters of God. His resurrection means that we are raised to His risen life, not to our old life. ". . . just as Christ was raised from the dead by the glory of the Father, even so we also should walk in newness of life . . . we also shall be in the likeness of His resurrection" (Romans 6:4-5).

Our Experiential Life

That I may know Him and the power of His resurrection, and the fellowship of His sufferings, being conformed to His death (Philippians 3:10; see also Romans 6:23).

Eternal life is not a present given to me by God, it is Himself. "The gift of God," not from God. How is the life of God going to work out in us? First of all, it will manifest itself in our mortal flesh in the way of death. The surging life of God instantly hates to death the things that have nothing to do with God. We experience exhaustion, a drying up of the springs of intellectual and physical life, the reason being that God is teaching us that all our life is now in the hand of God. Then the Holy Spirit will experientially reveal the power of His resurrection. If we are right with God, physical exhaustion will always bring its own recuperation. The exhaustion does not tell because He recuperates all the time. It is not a question of being buoyed up with excitement; it is a superabounding supply of life all the time. If we live in touch with our Lord's life experientially, we realize that our bodies are the temples of the Holy Spirit. This come to us first as a revelation, not as something to be experienced only. If we live on the experiential side alone, we shall get distracted. The resurrection of Jesus Christ has given Him the right, the authority, to impart the life of God to us, and our experiential life must be constructed on the basis of His life. "All my springs are in you" (Psalm 87:7).

Watch the things that exhaust you, and you will find you are doing something outside God's arrangement for us, the natural exhaustion is so quickly recuperated by the resurrection life of Jesus that we do not feel the exhaustion. We must find out whether we are instructing ourselves in the Christian revelation. Do we know the power of His resurrection? Are we making that the center of our profound life? If we are, the experiential reality will work throughout.

His Resurrection Deity

Jesus said to her, "Do not cling to Me, for I have not yet ascended to My Father; but go to My brethren and say to them, 'I am ascending to My Father and your Father, and to My God and your God' " (John 20:17).

The risen Lord as Son of Man is talking to a particular representative of humanity, the woman out of whom He has cast seven demons. Our Lord is the same, yet so indefinably altered by His death and resurrection that Mary did not recognize Him at first. Then when He said to her, "Mary," she flung herself at His feet with a complete thrill of expectancy. "He is back again, and all things will be well!" Mary had to learn that the relationship she was now to be in to with her Lord was not one that could be discerned by her natural senses, but a relationship based on an impartation of life from Himself. "I am ascending to my Father and your Father." It was to be a relationship in which she was made one with Jesus Christ. His resurrection deity means that He can take us into union with God, and the way into that relationship of oneness is by the cross and the resurrection. The weakest saint can experience the power of the deity of the Son of God if he is willing to "let go." The whole almighty power of God is on our behalf, and when we realize this, life becomes the implicit life of the child. No wonder Jesus said, "let not your heart be troubled!" The characteristic of the saintly life is abandon to God, not a settling down on our own "purity." God is not making hothouse plants, but sons and daughters of God, men and women with a strong family likeness to Jesus Christ.

Our Entire Life

If you were raised with Christ, seek those things which are above, where Christ is, sitting at the right hand of God. Set your mind on things above, not on things on the earth. For you died, and your life is hidden with Christ in God. When Christ who is our life appears, then you also will appear with Him in glory (Colossians 3:1-4).

We starve our minds as Christians by not thinking, and we cannot think as Christians until we are born from above. So many of us have a good spiritual experience, but we have never thought things out on Christian lines. It is just as true that a man may live a Christian life without thinking as that a man may think a Christian life without living it. We have to learn to combine the two, and to do this, we must build up our minds on these great truths.

If we have been born from above, we must seek the things that are above. To anyone who is not born from above, it sounds mystical and remote, but there is nothing too profound for a saint. We can always know a saint because he discerns the revelations of God, while the unspiritual man who has not been born from above looks puzzled. Truth is not discerned intellectually; it is discerned spiritually.

The power of the resurrection is to work out in these mortal bodies. Provided we are alive when our Lord comes again, we shall be changed, Paul says, and he goes on to expound the marvelous transformation that will take place in a flash in everything to do with the natural.

"Your life is hidden with Christ in God." Christ is our entire life. When once we realize this, certain forms of doubt and perplexity vanish forever. If we set our affection on things above, those perplexities will never trouble us anymore because we know the Lord Jesus, and He is not distracted by these present perplexities. The things that are obscure to the natural man become clear to the penetration of the mind that sets itself on the things above. Such a one does not pretend not to have doubts; we know he has not got them. His is not a stoical calm. The reason is that he has been living for a long time in Colossians 3, the entire life is hid with Christ in God, the whole set of the mind is on the things above, and the things on earth are transfigured.

Thank God that the almighty power of Jesus Christ is for us. All power is vested in Him in heaven and on earth, and He says, "Lo, I am with you always." All the power of the deity of Christ is ours through His resurrection.

His Ascension and Our Union

(Luke 24:50-51; Acts 1:9-10)

His Transfiguration Consummated
(John 17:5)
Our Supernatural Salvation (Acts 2:33)

His Transformation Completed
(Matthew 28:18)
Our Sanctified Security (John 14:13)

His Trustiness Continued (Acts 7:56)
Our Simple Satisfaction (John 17:23)

All the events in our Lord's life to which we have no corresponding experience happened after the transfiguration. From then onward, our Lord's life was altogether vicarious. Up to the time of the transfiguration, He had exhibited the normal perfect life of a man; from the transfiguration onward, everything is unfamiliar to us. Gethsemane, the cross, the resurrection—there is nothing like these experiences in our human life. From the transfiguration on, we are dealing not so much with the life our Lord lived as with the way He opened the door for us to enter into His life. At His ascension, our Lord enters heaven and keeps the door open for humanity. His cross is the door for every member of the human race to enter into the life of God.

Because of His resurrection, our Lord has the right to give eternal life to every individual (see John 17:2); by His ascension, He becomes the possessor of all power in heaven and in earth (see Matthew 28:18).

His Transfiguration Consummated

And now, O Father, glorify Me together with Yourself, with the glory which I had with You before the world was (John 17:5).

When our Lord as a man had fulfilled all God's demands of Him, and when by obedience He had transformed His natural life into a spiritual life, earth had no more hold on Him. On the Mount of Transfiguration, His real nature, that is, His essential deity, broke throughout the natural, and He was transfigured. He had fulfilled all the requirements of His Father for His earthly life, and God's presence, symbolized in the cloud, waited to usher Him back into the glory that He had with the Father before the world was. But He turned His back on the glory and came down from the mount to identify Himself with fallen humanity, because through Calvary there was to issue the newly constructed humanity. If Jesus Christ had gone to heaven from the Mount of Transfiguration, He would have gone alone. He would have been to us a glorious figure, One who manifested the life of God's normal man—and how wonderful it is for God and man to live as one—but what good would that have been to us? We can never live in the power of an ideal put before us. What is the use of Jesus Christ telling us we must be as pure in heart as He is when we know we are impure? But Jesus Christ did not go to heaven from the mount. Moses and Elijah talked with Him, not of His glory and not of His deity, but of His death—the issue that He was about to accomplish at Jerusalem. By His death on the cross, Jesus Christ made the way for every son of man to get into communion with God.

It was on this point that the enemy of God and of man assailed our Lord in the Garden of Gethsemane: "You will never get through as Son of Man; You will get through as deity, but not as deity incarnate." Our Lord's object in becoming deity incarnate was to redeem mankind, and He did get through as Son of Man, which means that any and every individual has freedom of access straight to God by right of the cross of Jesus Christ. That is regeneration being made effectual in human lives, and the Holy Spirit is the One who makes this marvelous redemption actual in us.

On the Mount of Ascension, the transfiguration is completed. There is a similarity in the details of the two scenes, because the ascension is the consummation of the transfiguration. Our Lord does now, without any hesitation, go back into His primal glory; He does now go straight to the fulfillment of all the transfiguration promised. But He does not go back simply as Son of God; He goes back to God as Son of Man as well as Son of God. The barriers are broken down, sin is done away with, death is destroyed, the power of the enemy is paralyzed, and there is now freedom of access for anyone straight to the very throne of God by the ascension of the Son of Man. As He ascended, our Lord stretched out His hands, the hands that He deliberately showed to the disciples after His resurrection, and the last the disciples saw of Him was His pierced hands. Those pierced hands are emblematic of the atonement, and the angels' declaration was that it is "this same Jesus" who is to come again, with the marks of the atonement upon Him. The atonement means that the whole of the human race has been atoned for—redemption is complete—and any person can get straight to the throne of God without let or hindrance through the wonder of all that our Lord has done. He is now at the right hand of the Father, not only as Son of God (see John 1:18), but as Son of Man.

Our Supernatural Salvation. "Therefore being exalted to the right hand of God, and having received from the Father the promise of the Holy Spirit, He poured out this, which you now see and hear" (Acts 2:33).

Salvation means the incoming into human nature of the great characteristics that belong to God, and there is no salvation that is not supernatural. It is easy to say that human love and divine love are one and the same thing; actually they are very far from being the same. It is also easy to say that human virtues and God's nature are one and the same thing, but this, too, is actually far from the truth. We must square our thinking with facts. Sin has come in and made a hiatus between human and divine love, between human virtues and God's nature, and what we see now in human nature is only the remnant and refraction of the divine. Human virtues according to the Bible are not promises of what human nature is going to be, but remnants of what human nature once was. This explains why we so often see remnants of original nobility in men and women who have not been born again into the kingdom of God. As Christians, we must learn to trace things to their right source. God makes very distinct the difference between the qualities that are divine and those that are human. John 15:13 has reference to human love, which lays down its life for its friends. Romans 5:8 has reference to the divine love, which lays down its life for its enemies, a thing human nature can never do. This does not mean that human beings cannot forgive; they can and do forgive. But forgiveness is not human, it belongs entirely to the divine nature and is a miracle when exhibited in the human.

Beware of philosophies. It is much more satisfactory to listen to a philosopher than to a proclaimer of the gospel, because the latter talks with the gibes and the cuts of God, and they go straight to that in man which hates the revelation of the gap there is between man and God. If we accept the revelation, it will mean that we must be born from above. And the gospel message is that we can be born from above the second we want to.

Intellectually, we are inclined to ignore sin. The one element in man that does not ignore sin is conscience. The Holy Spirit deals with conscience first, not with intellect or emotions. When the Holy Spirit gets hold of a person and convicts him of sin, he instantly gets to despair, for he recognizes that the holiness of Jesus Christ is the only thing that can ever stand before God, and he knows there is no chance for him. When conviction of sin comes in this way, there is only one of two places: suicide or the cross of Jesus Christ. The majority of us are shallow; we do not bother our heads about reality. We are taken up with actual comforts, with actual ease and peace, and when the Spirit of God comes in and disturbs the equilibrium of our life, we prefer to ignore what He reveals.

Salvation is always supernatural. The Holy Spirit brings me into union with God by dealing with that which broke the union. It is dangerous to preach a persuasive gospel, to try to persuade men to believe in Jesus Christ with the idea that if they do, He will develop them along the natural line. Jesus Christ said, "I did not come to bring peace but a sword." There is something to be destroyed first. Jesus Christ does not produce heaven and peace and delight straight off; He produces pain and misery and conviction and upset, and a person says, "If that is all He came to do, then I wish He had never come." But this is not at all what He came to do; He came to bring us into a supernatural union with His Father. When one believes in Jesus Christ; that is, commits himself to Jesus Christ (belief is a moral act, not an intellectual act), then the ascended Lord, by the Holy Spirit, brings the person into oneness with His Father. It is a supernatural union.

The two centers of Christian life are experience and revelation. Are we thinking along the line of the revelations Jesus Christ has given? We can never get into touch with God by our own effort, but we must maintain touch with God by our own effort (see Philippians 2:12-13). Jesus Christ can take anyone, no matter who he is, and presence him with His wonderful divine salvation. The nature of God is shed abroad in our hearts by the Holy Spirit, but we have to maintain contact with His nature by obedience. Some sections of the Christian community teach that because we are all right in the anticipation of God, therefore, it does not matter how we live actually. That is not true. We must not only be right in heart toward God, our life must show that we are right. Jesus Christ's life must work through our flesh, and that is where we have to obey. So many go into raptures over God's supernatural salvation, over the wonderful fact that God saves us by His sovereign grace (and we cannot do that too much), but they forget that now He expects us to get ourselves into trim to obey Him. We have to live in this mortal flesh as sons and daughters of God; we have to bring out to our fingertips the life that is hid with Christ in God, and we can do it because our ascended Lord has all power. If our flesh and blood does not allow the Son of God to manifest Himself in us, we are actually antichrist: We preach what our life denies; we proclaim a creed that our practical life spits at in ridicule. It is unconscious blasphemy to deny by our life that Jesus Christ can do what He claims He can. If we are born again, we are born into the life of God, and we have to see to it that we obey His life, and the faithfulness of the Holy Spirit is shown by the way He conscientiously chases us into a corner by touching every point where we have not been obeying.

His Transformation Completed

> Then Jesus came and spoke to them, saying, "All authority has been given to Me in heaven and on earth" (Matthew 28:18; see also Matthew 11:27).

In Matthew 11:27, our Lord states that the revelation of the Father is entirely confined to the Son, He is the only medium for revealing the Father. In Matthew 28:18 He says, "All authority has been given to Me in heaven and on earth." Then has He power to make a saint of me? If not, He has totally misunderstood Himself and has misled me. Has He all power on earth? What about this "piece of earth" I have to look after, has He power over it? Am I professing by my lips that I am a Christian while my actual "piece of earth" laughs to scorn what Jesus Christ says? He says, "All authority has been given to me." Am I demonstrating that He has no power at all?

As Son of Man, Jesus Christ deliberately limited omnipotence, omnipresence, and omniscience in Himself; now they are His in absolute full power. As deity, they were always His; now as Son of Man, they are His in absolute full power. At the throne of God, Jesus Christ has all power as Son of Man. That means He can do anything for any human being in keeping with His own character.

Our Sanctified Security. "And whatever you ask in my name, that I will do, that the Father may be glorified in the Son" (John 14:13). That is where our salvation abides in its perfect security. Couple with these words our Lord's other statement, "All power is given to me." You say, "Oh well, then I can ask anything I like." Try it! I defy you to do it. Our Lord says also, "Ask what you will, that is, what your will is in." There is very little our wills are in; consequently, it is easy to work up false emotions. When you have been touched by the Holy Spirit and have received His quickening, note what you evade in prayer. There is nothing that will detect spiritual rottenness quicker than to ask, that is, with the will. We shall find we have to stop asking a number of things, and this will simplify prayer. Our Lord says, "Ask," and we will always find that we do not ask when we talk about it. "I'll pray about it," but we won't. To say we will pray about a thing often means we are determined not to think about it. Contact with Jesus Christ made the disciples realize that they were paupers, and they said, ". . . Lord, teach us to pray . . ." (Luke 11:1).

If we are perplexed over the question of sanctification or about the baptism of the Holy Spirit, we ourselves are the reason why we are bothered. God has written a book and the phrases "sanctification" and the "baptism of the Holy Spirit" are His, not man's. Why do we not go to Him about it? We are the reason why we do not go; we dare not go. If we honestly ask God to baptize us with the Holy Spirit and fire, anything that happens is His answer, and some appalling things happen. If we accept the revelation that our body is the temple of the Holy Spirit, are we prepared to ask God to fulfill the purpose of the Holy Spirit in our body? If we are, watch the consequences—that friendship must go, that book, that association, every one of them must decay off like a lightning flash. If anyone has a difficulty in getting through to God, it is never God who is to blame. We can get through to Him as soon as we want to. There is nothing simpler. The trouble is when we begin to sympathize with the thing that is proud and strong in independence of God.

If we have been supernaturally saved by the redemption of Jesus Christ, we know we are unfit; therefore, we do not bother any more about ourselves, and as we walk in the light, we have perfect freedom of access into the very heart and presence of God. The life of communion with God that Jesus lived on earth is what He has made possible for us by His ascension.

Do not ask others to pray for you: our Lord says, "Pray yourself, ask." We each have our families, our Sunday School classes, our communities, our nation—how many of us are praying for them, or are we shirking the responsibility? We have to ask the thing that our will is in, and we cannot put our will into things God has not brought before us. "Whatever you ask in My name, that I will do." "In My name," not in Christian jargon, or in the piety of spurious devotion, but "in My nature." "The effective, fervent prayer of a righteous man avails much." The prayers of some people are more efficacious than those of others, the reason being that they are under no delusion, they do not rely on their own earnestness, they rely absolutely on the supreme authority of the Lord Jesus Christ (see Hebrews 10:19).

His Trustiness Continued

And [Stephen] said, "Look! I see the heavens opened and the Son of Man standing at the right hand of God" (Acts 7:56).

Stephen sees our Lord after His ascension, and He is the same Jesus (see Revelation 1:17-18). Some teach that the Jesus of actual history is not the Christ and that the risen Jesus is a conception of the divinely inspired imagination of the disciples. But it was "this same Jesus" that ascended—the marks of the atonement were upon Him. When we look for the characteristics of the ascended Lord in the accounts of the historic Jesus, we are on the right track. We will find His characteristics in the New Testament, and He will exhibit these same characteristics to us in almighty power.

Our Simple Satisfaction. "That they may be made perfect in one" (John 17:23). The baptism of the Holy Spirit delivers us from the husk of independent individuality. By personality is meant the thing in every individual that the Spirit of God awakens and brings out into real communion with God. Individual self-assertiveness is the husk; personal identity with our Lord is the kernel. Individuals can never be made one; persons can. Individuality is all "elbows," it separates and isolates. A child is an individual, and it ought to be independent. Our Lord can never be defined in terms of individuality and independence, but only in terms of personality. The thing that is marked throughout His life is personality, not independence and self-assertiveness. In the natural life when two people fall in love with one another, the individuality is transfigured because the personalities are merged. Identity is not domination but oneness between two distinct persons in which neither dominates, but the oneness dominates both. In the natural life if the individuality reasserts itself, there will be hitches and difficulties, and the same with the spiritual life. Jesus said,

"If you would be my disciples, you must deny yourself, give up your right to yourself to Me."

The natural independence of individuality springs from independence of God. If I will give up my right to myself to Him, the real true nature of my personality will answer to God straight away by the indwelling Holy Spirit. Jesus prayed, "that they may be one, as We are." When Paul urges us to put on the new man, he is urging on the most practical line that we put on in our actual life the habits that are in perfect accordance with the oneness with God, and that we do it all the time. Then there will come the simple satisfaction of knowing that God is answering the prayer of Jesus Christ. If you want to know what God is after in your life, read John 17. He prays that "they may be one, as We are." How close to God is Jesus Christ? "I and my Father are one." That is what He asks for us, and the Father will not leave us alone until the prayer is answered. Are we hindering the power of God in our life? Then never let us blame God. We may not only be supernaturally saved; we may be supernaturally sanctified. If we will submit to God and obey Him, we shall know that all that the Lord Jesus is in Himself is ours straightaway with the greatest ease and power and satisfaction by the right of His ascension. He is King of Kings and Lord of Lords from the day of His ascension until now.

His Glorification and Ours

His Former Form of God (John 17:5)
Our Present Glorying (Galatians 6:14)

His Fulfilled Fitness in God (1 Corinthians 15:28)
Our Prevailing Glory (Romans 8:30)

His Faithful Face of God (John 1:14)
Our Perpetual Glory (John 17:24)

As already stated, we must have Christian experience, but we must have more. Many of us are kindly interested in Christianity and in being devoted to Jesus Christ, but we have never received anything from Him. If we told ourselves the truth, we could not say that God had regenerated us experientially. If we are not to be merely sentimental Christians, we must know what it is to be born into the kingdom of God and to find out that God has altered the things that matter to us. That must be made perfectly clear first, and we have the experience described in Acts 26:18. We must have the experience of the new life, and then we have to see that the new life is instructed by the facts in God's Book. There are things that we cannot experience as Christians, yet we must build our faith upon them and not choose according to the predilections that are the outcome of our own experience.

174

His Former Form of God

And now, O Father, glorify Me together with
Yourself, with the glory which I had with You
before the world was (John 17:5).

Jesus Christ came from somewhere to here, and the
"somewhere" whence He came was absolute deity. Jesus
Christ was not a being who became divine, He was the
Godhead incarnated: "who, being in the form of God . . . ."
The "form" of God originally in absolute deity is not the
form we understand by the body, but "glory," the
completeness of God, a form inconceivable to our human
minds in which what we call the Trinity was an
absoluteness. The term "Trinity" is not a Bible word, but a
term that arose in the throes of a great conflict of minds and
is the crystallized attempt to state the Godhead in a word.
One element of the Godhead became, through the Word of
God, the incarnate Son of God. Beware of separating God
manifest in the flesh from the Son becoming sin. In other
words, never separate the doctrine of the incarnation and
the doctrine of redemption. The New Testament reveals
that God became incarnate only for the purpose of putting
away sin. God did not become incarnate for the purpose of
self-revelation.

When the Son of God, who became Son of Man, has done
His work, He will be resolved back again into absolute deity
(see 1 Corinthians 15:28; John 17:5). This is where our
vocabulary will not go. We get into difficulties over God
becoming incarnate when we bring in our own conceptions.
For instance, we say that the essential nature of God is
omnipotence, omnipresence, and omniscience; the New
Testament reveals that the essential nature of God is holiness

and that He became the weakest thing in His own creation—a baby. Are we prepared to abandon our own conceptions? We are all idolaters; we do mentally what Isaiah ridiculed the people in his day for doing (see Isaiah 44:9-20). Our ideas have no more power over us than we choose to give them. We bring God to the bar of the judgment of our ideas. Jesus Christ said that His Father made His revelations to babes. Are we modest enough, and humble enough, and regenerate enough to accept Him as master of our brains as well as of our souls? Are we willing to be as submissive to incarnate reason as we are to incarnate God? Incarnate reason is the Lord Jesus, and any man who exercises his reason in contradiction to incarnate reason is a fool. We must never take our Lord's words and interpret them by our own human reason; we must always interpret them by His life. Am I prepared to be a believer in Jesus Christ? To believe in Jesus means much more than the experience of salvation in any form: It entails a mental and moral commitment to our Lord's view of the world, of the flesh, of the devil, of God, of man, and of the Scriptures. To "believe also in Me" means that we submit our intelligence to His Father. This does not mean that we do not exercise our reason, but it does mean that we exercise it in submission to reason incarnate.

"And now, O Father, glorify Me with Yourself, with the glory which I had with You before the world was" (John 17:5). Our Lord is referring to the former form of God. No human being has any conception of what that is; it is a revelation. The insidious teaching abroad today, the heresy that dissolves the person of Jesus Christ, has crept in everywhere. Jesus Christ asks in His prayer, from His position as Son of Man, that He might be taken back to His former glory. "I have finished the work which You have given Me to do." What was the work? To rehabilitate the human race, to bring the human race back to God—that is the work that God has given Him to do. Jesus Christ made the way clear for man to get straight into at-one-ment with God. Now that that work is completed—completed in His will and soon to be completed in actuality—our Lord prays that He may be in the former form of God. There is no human connection in His prayer; it is superbly divine.

Is Jesus Christ to me what He is in His estimate of Himself? He makes the destiny of the whole human race depend upon their relationship to Him. It is not the divinity but the deity of Jesus Christ that is the important thing.

Our Present Glorying. "But God forbid that I should glory except in the cross of our Lord Jesus Christ, by whom the world has been crucified to me, and I to the world" (Galatians 6:14). Glorying is the experience of joy on the inside associated with the fame of God on the outside. Paul says his glorying is in the cross of Christ, "and God forbid that I should glory in any other thing." Joy is neither happiness nor brightness; joy is literally the nature of God in my blood, no matter what happens. The joy that Jesus exhibited in His life was in knowing that every power of His nature was in harmony with His Father's nature; therefore, He did with delight what God designed Him for as Son of Man. Anything that exactly fulfills the purpose of its creation experiences joy, and Paul states that our joy is that we fulfill the purpose of God in our lives by being saints. How are we going to be saints? We all like to listen to the life of Jesus and to His teaching, but what does it all amount to? Ask the one who has been born again, and he will tell you, to the limit of his language, the difference it has made. It has made an absolute difference, because by the cross of Jesus Christ, we enter into the life of the Son of God. What is the sign that we are born from above? That we see the rule of God. Have we got in us the new power, the new life, the new disposition that actually works itself out in our actual life? Our Lord did not tell us to ask for peace or for joy or for life; He told us to ask for the Holy Spirit (Luke 11:13), and when we ask, the honor of Jesus Christ is at stake. The reason God gives us the Holy Spirit so easily is because of what His Son has done, and yet He never emphasizes what it cost; that is in the background altogether.

Our glorying is in the cross of Jesus Christ because it is through this doorway that all the new life comes in (see 1 Corinthians 2:2). The normal life that God wants us to live is the life of the Lord Jesus Christ, but what good does it do us to talk about the speckless perfection of Jesus Christ? It would be a tantalizing thing if all Jesus Christ gave us was the example of His own life. If a person is in earnest, it produces absolute despair. What is the good of teaching the Beatitudes, the Sermon on the Mount? They are out of our reach altogether. Once we remember that the normal life, the life of perfect oneness with God, is ours by means of Jesus Christ's death, it is all explained. We can enter there by His cross. Have we entered there? It does not matter who the man is, how degraded or how moral, he can enter in at the door of His death and then never cease to thank God that this is the crown of his joy. It is through the cross of Jesus Christ that we begin to fulfill all that we are created for, and the great aim of the life is for the fame of God, not for the needs of men. Human sympathy has swamped the commands of God in the average Christian. Instead of the need being the opportunity, it is made to be the call. The first of all the commandments is "You shall love the Lord your God with all your heart, with all your soul, with all your mind, and with all your strength."

The basis of reality is redemption and not reason. Reason is the basis of the way we work on reality, it is an instrument. Thank God for logic and for reason, they are instruments for expressing our life, but life itself is not reasonable. Man's intellect has no power to lead him; his intellect makes him either a polished hypocrite or, in the case of a disciple of Jesus Christ, it becomes the bond slave of the right discernment of God's will (see John 7:17).

His Fulfilled Fitness in God

Now when all things are made subject to Him, then the Son Himself will also be subject to Him who put all things under Him, that God may be all in all (1 Corinthians 15:28).

This is the fulfillment of the prayer in John 17:5. When the redemption wrought by the Son is actually fulfilled and all things are subdued unto Him, and when the whole human race and God are at one, then the Son of Man will cease to be by resolving back again into absolute deity. "Now when all things are made subject to Him"— remember everything is not yet subdued unto Him. Redemption does not only mean personal salvation and the redemption of our body; it means the absolute and complete redemption of the whole material earth in every iota, and not only the earth, but the whole material universe: "a new heaven and a new earth." It means that all relegated authority shall pass, and God will be the absolute authority: "That God may be all in all." There is a time coming, thank God, when everything shall be under the direct rule of God in every detail. We look for a new heaven and a new earth, and then will the human race stand before God as Jesus

Christ stood before Him when He was here. Jesus Christ, Son of God and Son of Man, is not a mere individual; He is the One who represents the whole human race. To see the human race as God intends it to be, look at the life of Jesus, and by the redemption the human race is to be brought there. When the human race is actually there, Jesus Christ as Son of Man ceases to be and becomes absolute deity again. The Son becomes subject to the Father, and God remains all in all. Our Lord's prayer is answered. "And now, O Father, glorify Me with Yourself, with the glory which I had with You before the world was." That glory is to be in God.

Our Prevailing Glory. "And whom He justified, these He also glorified" (Romans 8:30). In John 17:5 we see the transcendent revelation of the absolute deity of our Lord; in John 17:22 He speaks of a second glory: "And the glory which You gave Me I have given them." What glory had Jesus when He became the Son of Man vicariously, when He became the whole human race in one person? What was His glory then? Did everyone who saw Him say, "That is God incarnate?" No, Isaiah said He shall be "as a root out of a dry ground," utterly disadvantaged. Is this true? Look in your own heart and you will see it is true. "He has no form or comeliness; and when we see Him, there is no beauty that we should desire Him." It is not true that "we needs must love the highest when we see it." The human beings of His own day saw the Highest, and they hated Him. It needs the transformation of an inward surgery, being born from above, to see that He is the altogether lovely One. The glory of Jesus was not an external thing; He effaced the Godhead in Himself so effectually that men without the Spirit of God despised Him. His glory was the glory of actual holiness. What is holiness? Transfigured morality blending with indwelling God. Any other kind of holiness is fictitious and dangerous. One of the dangers of dealing too much with the higher Christian life is that it is apt to fizzle off into abstractions. But when we see holiness in the Lord Jesus, we do know what it means, it means an unsullied thinking of the mind, unsullied transactions of the bodily organs, unsullied life of the heart, unsullied dreams of the imagination: That is the actual holiness Jesus says He has given them. This is the meaning of sanctification. Paul says, and no wonder, "My little children, for whom I labor in birth again until Christ is formed in you." The holiness of the Son of God is to be actually manifested in our ordinary bodily lives. This is the actual experience of sanctification working out in each detail.

This is our prevailing glory; Paul is not talking about being justified and glorified hereafter, but now. Thank God, the joy of the Lord is an actual experience now, and it goes beyond any conscious experience, because the joy of the Lord takes us into the consciousness of God, and the honor at stake in our body is the honor of God. Have we realized that the Son of God has been formed in us by His wonderful redemption? Are we putting on the habits that are in keeping with Him? This is the glory of the saint here and now—the glory of actual holiness manifested in actual life. Whether it comes out in eating and drinking or in preaching, it must show in every detail straight through until the whole limit actually manifests the complete new life.

His Faithful Face of God

And the Word became flesh and dwelt among us, and we beheld His glory, the glory as of the only begotten of the Father, full of grace and truth (John 1:14).

In Genesis 1:2-3, we read that the Spirit of God brooded, the word of God was spoken, and creation was begun. John takes us back there (see Proverbs 8). The word has become incarnate in the Lord Jesus Christ. He is the word of God incarnated, made flesh, and in Him we see the face of God. All that our Lord said about Himself is in perfect accordance with this: "I and My Father are one." He did not say, "I and humanity are one." Jesus nowhere taught that God was in man, but He did teach that God was manifested in human flesh in His own person that He might become the generating center for the same thing in every human being. The place of His travail pangs is the incarnation and Calvary and the resurrection. Jesus Christ did not say that human beings were all specimens of God, as some men try to prove from conceptions of their own. "Reason being God, there can be nothing unreasonable; sin is not a positive thing, it is a defect in the desire to grasp hold of God." These blasphemies start from a thing that looks so humble, "God is all." God is not all. I am not God, neither are you. Jesus Christ reveals God as the Father. "I am the way . . . no one comes to the Father except through Me." Jesus Christ is not the way to God, not a road we leave behind us, a fingerprint that points in the right direction; He is the way itself. "Abide in me," consequently, the Lord satisfies the last aching abyss of the human heart. Has He satisfied yours? If not, why are you in Christian work? What is the explanation of the great craving for the salvation of the souls of men? If it is not born of the Holy Spirit experientially realized in us, it is nothing in the world but the introduction of sordid commercialism into religion (see Matthew 23:15). Why do we want people to be saved? Has Jesus Christ made such a difference to us that we cannot rest day or night till by prayer we get all our friends there? That is the passion for souls born of the Holy Spirit because its experiential reality is with us every day.

If we want to know what God is like, let us study the Lord Jesus. "He who has seen Me has seen the Father." How did people see Him in the days of His flesh? By their natural eyes? No, after His resurrection they received Holy Spirit, and their eyes were opened and they knew Him. We do not know Him by the reasoning of our minds, but by the new life. Jesus Christ is to us the faithful face of God. Could anyone be in doubt any more after they had seen Jesus Christ by the Holy Spirit? Think of the absurd, painful, distressing, never-to-be-answered questions we ask: "Shall I know those whom I love after death?" Wild, vagrant, wrong, stupid, painful questions. Look at Jesus Christ, get into contact with Him by the Holy Spirit, and those questions are impossible. He says, "Let not your heart be troubled; you believe in God, believe also in Me." The face of God is the Lord Jesus Christ. It always comes back to the simple point, "Come to Me."

Our Perpetual Glory. "Father, I desire that they also whom You gave Me may be with Me where I am, that they may behold My glory which You have given Me" (John 17:24). Now our Lord is speaking of the glory that we are only to behold. We are not to be absorbed into God as drops in an ocean; we are to be lifted into perfect oneness with Him until God and the glory of perfected human redemption are transfigured by a mutual love. "I desire that they also whom You gave Me," says Jesus, "may behold My glory." What is His glory? "The glory which I had with You before the world was," and our perpetual glory is not only that we are saved and sanctified and redeemed and lifted into the glory of unspeakable things as the result of our Lord's redemption, but something other—we shall see God face-to-face, an inconceivable beatific vision. This is what Jesus Christ has prayed for His saints. This is not the glory we have here, but the glory we are going to have, the glory of beholding His glory.

The Kenosis

Self-Limitation on the Part of the Logos in the Act of Incarnation

At one time the subject of the Kenosis was always being discussed by theologians: What was it that Jesus emptied Himself of? How did He limit Himself? Or did He limit Himself at all? Nowadays, the subject is scarcely touched upon; according to the modern standpoint Jesus Christ was simply a great, noble, and good man. It is not stated in so many words, but we are brought to that conclusion. We are told that by understanding our own consciousness, we can understand the consciousness of Jesus Christ. The New Testament reveals that to be false. Jesus distinctly said, "No one knows the Son, except the Father," and over and over again our Lord makes statements about Himself that reveal Him to be a unique Being.

The doctrine of the Kenosis is clear first to our heart, not to our head; it is a spiritual fact, not a thought-out fact. When a man's heart is right with God, the mysterious utterances of the Bible are "spirit and life" to him. Spiritual truth is discernible only to a pure heart, not to a keen intellect. It is not a question of profundity of intellect, but of purity of heart.

Self-Disglorification

Let this mind be in you which was also in Christ
Jesus, who, being in the form of God, did not
consider it robbery to be equal with God, but made
Himself of no reputation, taking the form of a
servant . . . (Philippians 2:5-7).

Paul does not tell us what Jesus emptied Himself of: He
emptied Himself of what He was in His former existence.
That is a revelation fact, and we must beware of any
explanation that explains it away. The apostle Paul does not
say that Jesus thought nothing of Himself. He thought
truthfully of Himself; He knew who He was. But there was
no self-assertion. Paul connects the two—being "equal with
God" and making "Himself of no reputation." That means
Jesus never presumed on His equality with God; He did not
continually assert it. There was only one brilliant moment in
the life of Jesus, and that was on the Mount of
Transfiguration. We do not know what the glory was that
He had with the Father before the world was, but if we
stand with Him on the Mount, we see what He emptied
Himself of. On the Mount the voice of the Father expressed
the divine approval: "This is my beloved Son, in whom I am
well pleased." Yet it was a step on to the cross—a way none
ever went before, or has ever had to go since.

Recall the temptation of our Lord. Satan tempted Him
on this very line—that is, to assert Himself. "Remember
who You are, the Son of God. Assert your prerogative as
Son." At the heart of every one of our Lord's answers is this:
"I did not come here to assert who I am; I came here for
God's will to be done through Me in His way."

The same temptation comes to us as God's children: "If

you are sanctified, presume on it. Think of it as something to be grasped." Whenever we get our thoughts fixed on our experience instead of on the God who gave us the experience, it is impossible to form the mind that was in Christ Jesus. It is not a question of sanctification, but of what happens after sanctification. The steadfast habit of the Christian life is the effacement of self, letting Jesus work through us without hindrance as the Father worked through Him.

Whenever we are told by the Spirit of God to follow the example of Jesus, the following is emphatically prescribed to a particular point:

> For to this you were called, because Christ also suffered for us, leaving us an example, that you should follow His steps; who committed no sin, nor was guile found in His mouth; who, when He was reviled, did not revile in return; when He suffered, He did not threaten . . . (1 Peter 2:21-23).

Peter makes it perfectly clear and unambiguous how we are to "follow His steps"—that is, in the way we suffer as Christians: ". . . who committed no sin, nor was guile found in His mouth . . . when He suffered, he did not threaten."

"Follow His example there," says Peter. Just as Christ exhibited an unthreatening spirit when He suffered, we are to do the same. No human being can suffer wrongfully without finding the spirit of threatening awakened in him, a spirit that if put into words would be, "I'll make that person smart! The idea of saying that about me!" If we are born again of the Holy Spirit, the disposition of Jesus in us will enable us to "follow His steps" so that when we suffer wrongfully, we do not threaten.

The following is distinctly limited to that one point: "Learn from Me; for I am gentle and lowly in heart." We are never told to be like the unique Being, the Lord Jesus Christ, who came into the world as God incarnate to put away sin. But when sin has been put away through the atonement, we are to be conformed to His image. To follow His steps does not mean we have the belittling idea that we are to be Jesus Christ over again. It is not a question of "What would Jesus do?" but "What would Jesus have me do?" We have to exhibit over again the life He exhibited—in this particular instance, in the circumstance of suffering wrongfully. Suffering is the touchstone of saintliness, just as temptation is, and suffering wrongfully will always reveal the ruling disposition, because it takes us unawares.

"Let this mind be in you, which was also in Christ Jesus." In this verse Paul indicates the kind of mind we are to form—that is, the mind of true humility, the mind of Christ that He exhibited when He was on earth, utterly self-effaced and self-emptied, not the mind of Christ when He was in glory. If you are a saint, says Paul, manifest it by having the mind that was in Christ who said, "I am among you as the One who serves."

One of the essential elements of deity is the humility expressed in a baby and in Jesus Christ. "And Jesus called a little child to Him, and set him in the midst of them, and said, 'Assuredly I say to you, unless you are converted and become as little children, you will by no means enter the kingdom of heaven.'" To interpret these words to mean that we are ideally to be servants of all would end in mock humility. We cannot form the mind of Christ if we do not have His Spirit, nor can we interpret His teaching apart from His Spirit.

Our spiritual destitution and entire dependence upon

God, and our despair of ever attaining to this kind of life, is in reality the most glorious chance for God. The Spirit of God never allows the thought that is apt to crop up now and again in spiritual teaching that we are to be specimens of what God can do. That thought is inspired by the devil, never by the Spirit of God. I am not here to be a specimen of what God can do; I am here to live the life so hid with Christ in God that what Jesus said will be true: "Men . . . may see your good works and glorify your Father in heaven."

Self-Renunciation

And the Word became flesh . . . (John 1:14).

For He made Him who knew no sin to be sin for us, that we might become the righteousness of God in Him (2 Corinthians 5:21).

The Word, the Logos, became flesh for one purpose: to be identified with sin and put it away. At His baptism our Lord took on Himself His vocation, which was to bear away the sin of the world, and it was along that line that He narrowed and limited and confined Himself. We miss the mark when we think on the aesthetic line and take our Lord as a specimen of a highly strung, superbly fine nature, suffering from contact with coarse natures. We are talking nonsense if we put His suffering there. He never paid the remotest attention to that kind of suffering, nor is there any allusion made to it in the New Testament. His suffering is not the suffering of a man of refined sensibilities among brutes, of a holy character among unholy characters.

His suffering is in a totally different domain and along a

different line from anything from which we suffer. It is the suffering of a Savior. "Though he was a Son, yet He learned obedience by the things which He suffered." Jesus Christ was God incarnate for one purpose: not to reveal God to us (that is simply one of the outcomes of the incarnation), but to bring back the whole human race into oneness with God. He who was "originally in the form of God," on an equality with God—which was His right, not a thing to be grasped—renounced it all, took upon Himself the form of a slave, and became obedient unto death, even the death of the cross, in order that He might deliver the weak and ungodly and sinful from sin (see Romans 5:6-8).

In presenting the life of Jesus Christ we are not presenting an example, but a historical fact essential to our soul's salvation. A sinner saved by grace will always refer in his testimony to the moment when he experienced new birth. People who have never been convicted of sin say that what we call saintliness is simply the evolution of the finer qualities in man. There is no room whatever for that thinking in the New Testament. The finer qualities of man are remnants and ruins of what he once was, not the promise of what he is going to be, and the only way a man can fulfill God's purpose is by being born from above. "Do not marvel that I said to you, 'You must be born again.'"

We have to be careful of the teaching built on the idea that Jesus Christ is a great, high and wonderful figure for us to imitate. There is no place in the New Testament for that idea. Unless we come to know Him as Savior, we are left amazingly unsatisfied—a beautiful influence, a wonderful life, that is all. "I did not come to call the righteous, but sinners." A sinner—that is, one convicted of sin—is the only one in a fit state to understand why Jesus came.

When God became incarnate in Jesus Christ for the

purpose of removing sin, people saw nothing in Him to desire. Jesus Christ is at a disadvantage in the eyes of everyone not convicted of sin: "He has no form or comeliness; and when we see Him, there is no beauty that we should desire Him." But when once the heart of a sinner is reached, that is a state of heart and mind able to understand why it was necessary for God to become incarnate. The worst state a person could be in is never to have had a twinge of conviction of sin, everything happy and peaceful, but absolutely dead to the realm of things Jesus represents.

Self-Expenditure

> For you know the grace of our Lord Jesus Christ, that though He was rich, yet for your sakes He became poor, that you through His poverty might become rich (2 Corinthians 8:9).

Grace is a "theological" word—unfortunately so, because we usually mean by theology something remote that has to do with controversy, whereby our mind is tied up in knots and our practical life left alone. In the Bible, theology is immensely practical. Grace means the overflowing nature of God. We see it in nature; we have no words to describe the lavishness of God. "The grace of our Lord Jesus Christ" is the overflowing of God's nature in entire and absolute forgiveness through His own sacrifice. Do we discern that grace? We talk about the sacrifice of the Son of God and forget that it was the sacrifice of God Himself. "God was in Christ, reconciling the world to Himself."

" . . . that you through His poverty might become rich." Rich in what? Not in possessions, but in personal identity.

Our Lord Jesus Christ became poor, not as an example, but to give us the secret of His religion. The religion of Jesus Christ is a religion of personal relationship to God and has nothing to do with possessions. Professional Christianity is a religion of possessions that are devoted to God. The disciple realizes that his life does not consist in the abundance of things he possesses, because what we possess often possesses us; we are possessed by possessions. "This is mine; you must not touch it!" When we become rich toward God, it will show in the details of our actual life.

"Without shedding of blood there is no remission." This is true of the marvelous redemption of our Lord Jesus, and true also of us as saints. The blood of the majority of Christians flows in hard cash. If ever we are to be loosened from the thing that keeps us poor in relation to God, we must shed our blood right out. "As having nothing, and yet possessing all things." The poverty of God's children in all ages is a significant thing, and the poverty has to come through calamity.

The Plerosis

The Self-Fulfilling of Jesus

We have to place the Lord Jesus Christ in relation to our faith where the New Testament places Him. We are apt to look upon Jesus Christ as some marvelous power of God with no identity of its own, forgetting altogether that the New Testament Jesus Christ, who transforms human lives by the miracle of regeneration, retains His own identity all through. Our Lord had a self-conscious existence built on exactly the same basis as our human personality.

What is true of the conscious and unconscious mind is true also of personality. The part of our personality of which we are conscious is the tiniest bit; underneath are the deep realms of unconscious life known only to God. Our Lord can never be defined in terms of individuality, but only in terms of personality: "I and my Father are one." Every bit of the personality of Jesus, conscious and unconscious, fulfilled the purpose of God.

His Sovereign Self-Identification

That they may be one just as We are one (John 17:22).

The Joy of Personality. "These things I have spoken to you, that My joy may remain in you, and that your joy might be full" (John 15:11). You can never use the word happiness in connection with Jesus or His disciples. It is an insult to God and to human nature to have as our ideal a happy life. Happiness is a thing that comes and goes; it can never be an end in itself. Holiness, not happiness, is the end of man.

The great design of God in the creation of man is that he might "glorify God and enjoy Him forever." A man never knows joy until he gets rightly related to God. Satan's claim is that he can make a man satisfied without God, but all he succeeds in doing is giving happiness and pleasure, never joy. Our lives mean much more than we can tell; they fulfill some purpose of God about which we know nothing. Our part is to "trust in the Lord with all your heart, and not lean on your own understanding." Earthly wisdom can never come near the threshold of the divine; if we stop short of the divine we stop short of God's purpose for our lives.

". . . that My joy may remain in you." What was the joy of Jesus? The joy of Jesus was the absolute surrender and sacrifice of Himself to the will of His Father, the joy of doing exactly what the Father sent Him to do. "I delight to do Your will." And He prays that His disciples may have this joy fulfilled in themselves.

There is no joy in a personality unless it can create. The joy of an artist is not in the fame that his pictures bring him, but that his work is the creation of his personality. The work of Jesus is the creation of saints; He can take the worst, the most misshapen material, and make a saint. "Therefore if anyone is in Christ, he is a new creation." The fullest meaning of sanctification is that Jesus Christ is "made unto us sanctification"—that is, He creates in us what He is Himself. The apostle Paul alludes to the joy of creating when he says, "For what is our hope, or joy, or crown of rejoicing? Is it not even you . . . ? For you are our glory and joy" (1 Thessalonians 2:19-20).

". . . who for the joy that was set before him endured the cross . . . ." It was not reward our Lord looked forward to, but joy. Reward is our lame word for joy. When we want a child to do well, we do not say, "You will have joy"; we say, "You will get a reward, a prize." The way the joy of Jesus manifests itself is that there is no desire for praise. As Bergson has pointed out, we want praise only when we are not sure of having done well; when we are certain we have done well, we don't care an atom whether folks praise us or not.

The Peace of Personality. "My peace I give to you" (John 14:27). The idea of peace in connection with personality is that every power is in perfect working order to the limit of activity. That is what Jesus means when He says "My peace." Never connect the idea of stagnation or being jaded with peace. Health is physical peace, but it is not stagnation; health is the perfection of physical activity. Virtue is moral peace, but it is not innocence; virtue is the perfection of moral activity. Holiness is spiritual peace, but it is not quietness; holiness is the most intense spiritual activity.

It is easy to conceive of a personality full of joy and peace, but isolated. The striking thing about our Lord is that He was never isolated. "If anyone loves me," He said, "We will come to him, and make our home with him." The conception is that of perfect converse and union; the abiding of the Trinity with the saint. The destiny of mankind in the purpose of God is not to do something, but to be something; "that they may be one even as We are."

Jesus had joy and peace to the last reach of His personality. With us it is possible to have joy and peace in one domain, and disturbance and unrest in another. We have

spells of joy and spells that are the opposite of joy—
tribulation that brings distress; but there is a time coming
when there will be no more tribulation, no more distress,
when every part of our personality will be as full of joy and
peace as was the Leader of our faith.

Do we have the unfathomable comfort of knowing that
in and above all the clouds and mysteries, the joy of Jesus is
unsullied? "Now to him that is able to keep you from
stumbling, and to present you faultless before the presence
of His glory with exceeding joy" (Jude 24). It is a good thing
to let the Spirit of God kindle our imagination as to what
Jesus Christ is able to do.

His Sovereign Self-Fulfillment

Therefore being exalted by the right hand of God . . .
(Acts 2:33).

The ascension placed Jesus Christ back in the glory that
He had with the Father before the world was. That is why
the ascension, not the resurrection, is the completion of the
transfiguration. The two visitants on the Mount, who might
well have come to usher Him back into heaven, instead spoke
with Him "of His decease which He was about to accomplish
at Jerusalem." "Now it came to pass, while He blessed them,
that He was parted from them and was carried up into
heaven," and the angels told the watching disciples that "this
same Jesus, who was taken up from you into heaven, will so
come in like manner as you saw Him go into heaven." Our
Lord does now, without any hesitation, go back into His
primal glory; but He does not go alone. Through His death
and resurrection He has made the way for the whole human
race to get to the very throne of God.

The death of Jesus was an enactment of the judgment of God upon the sin of the human race; the resurrection is the absolution of God pronounced upon the human race, the abolishing of death which is the wages of sin. By His resurrection our Lord has not only the right to give His own life to anyone who will take it, but power to "fashion anew the body of our humiliation, that it may be conformed to the body of his glory . . . ." That does not take place in this dispensation. Beyond our comprehension, you say? Only beyond the comprehension of intellect. There is all the difference between the comprehension of intellect and the comprehension of spirit. We comprehend a thing by our spirit and feel we know it but cannot express it; it is a knowledge "which surpasses all understanding."

Supreme Power. "All authority has been given to Me in heaven and on earth" (Matthew 28:18). All authority is given—to whom? To the Being who lived a humble, obscure life in Nazareth; to the One who says, "Come to me, all you who labor and are heavy laden, and I will give you rest."

If all power is given to Jesus Christ, what right have I to insult Him by worrying? If we will let these words of Jesus come into our hearts, we will soon see how contemptible our unbelief is. Jesus Christ will do anything for us in keeping with His own character; the power that comes from Him is stamped with His nature. Will I say skeptically, "What does Jesus Christ know about my circumstances? Are His power and understanding sufficient to manage things for me?" To talk like that is the way to realize the size of our unbelief, and to see why Jesus Christ was so stern in condemning it.

"All authority has been given to Me." And yet Paul says, "He was crucified in weakness," and he adds that "we also are weak in Him." Am I powerful enough to be weak? Any weak man can strike another back; it requires a strong man to take it meekly. The omnipotence of Jesus at work in a man means that neither the world, the flesh, nor the devil can make him show anything but Christlikeness. The self-identification of Jesus with His servants through all the ages is along this line: "They realized that they had been with Jesus."

The meaning of salvation in experience is that we are enabled to manifest in our mortal flesh the family likeness that Jesus had to God. There is only one kind of humanity and one kind of holiness—the holiness manifested in the life of the Lord Jesus; and it is that holiness that He gives to us. It is not that we are put in a place where we are like Him. In Galatians 2:20 the apostle Paul refers to the fact that the very disposition of holiness that was in Jesus is in him, too, by means of identification with Jesus' death. It is not sentiment, it is a fact; not poetry, but a practical working-out of this marvelous likeness to Jesus Christ. "We know that when He is revealed, we shall be like Him; for we shall see Him as He is" (1 John 3:2).

Supreme Wisdom. "Whatever you ask in My name, that I will do" (John 14:13). When you pray, remember that it is Jesus Christ who carries out the answer; God hands over this marvelous power to Him. By His ascension our Lord became omniscient, all-wise. Have we ever had a glimpse of what that means? The wisdom He exercised in a limited sphere, and in complete dependence on His Father while on earth, He now exercises in an unlimited sphere.

The revelation of our spiritual standing is what we ask in prayer. Sometimes what we ask is an insult to God; we ask with our eyes on the possibilities or on ourselves, not on Jesus Christ. Get onto the supernatural line. Remember that

Jesus Christ is omniscient, and He says, "Whatever you ask in My name, I will do it.

Supreme Presence. "And lo, I am with you always." Don't refine this revelation fact away by taking it to mean a spiritual presence by the Holy Spirit. It is a grander, more massive revelation than that; "I am with you always." Through His ascension the glorified Lord is with us always. May God lift the veil as to what this means. Who was it who saw Jesus after the resurrection? Only those who had spiritual insight. When the Spirit of God opens our spiritual eyes, we see Jesus "crowned with glory and honor."

By His ascension our Lord raised Himself to glory; He became omnipotent, omniscient, and omnipresent. All the splendid power, so circumscribed in His earthly life, became omnipotence; all the wisdom and insight, so precious but limited during His life on earth, became omniscience; all the unspeakable comfort of His presence, so confined to a few in His earthly life, became omnipresence; He is with us all the days.

What kind of Lord Jesus do we have? Is He the all-powerful God in our present circumstances, in our providential setting? Is He the all-wise God of our thinking and our planning? Is He the ever-present God, "closer than breathing, nearer than hands or feet?" If He is, we know what it means to "abide under the shadow of the Almighty." No one can tell us where the shadow of the Almighty is; we have to find it out for ourselves.

When by obedience we have discovered where it is, we must abide there—"No evil shall befall you, nor shall any plague come near your dwelling." That is the life that is more than conqueror because the joy of the Lord has become its strength; and that soul is on the way to entering ultimately into the joy of the Lord.

Our Lord's View of Himself and His Work—I

The Fact of Christ

"But whom do you say that I am?" Jesus Christ is not a Being with a dual personality, He is a unique personality with two manifestations: Son of God and Son of Man. He gives clear indication of how He lived a holy life, of how He thought and spoke, and He also gives clear expositions of God. Those expositions were given in a human body like ours, and the New Testament reveals how it is possible for us to live the same kind of life that Jesus lived through the marvel of the atonement, because the disposition that ruled Him is ruling us. What God demands of us is the very holiness Jesus Christ exhibited in His life. We can "follow His steps" by recognizing the wonderful work He has done, and manifest daily the marvel of His grace.

The first thing we have to do is clear away the difficulties that have gathered around the fact of Christ.

Intellectual Difficulties

Preconceptions. "Being (as was supposed) the son of Joseph" (Luke 3:23). There were many preconceptions about our Lord in His day, and this was a prevalent one. We do not bring with us these preconceptions, but we bring others. We have made up our mind that God will come only along certain lines, and when He comes on another line, we, like the religious people of His day, do not recognize Him. It is difficult for anyone brought up with religious conceptions to get rid of them in the right way.

What mental conception do we bring with us when we come to study the Lord Jesus Christ? If, for instance, a person has an agnostic preconception, it will obscure everything the New Testament says about God becoming incarnate. This preconception may not trouble us, but it is well to recognize that such a preconception exists. An agnostic says, "I cannot accept anything about deity; I can accept only facts about human nature." If you tell him he must accept the fact that Jesus Christ is the Son of God, you will never get near him; but if you go on this line—"Do you believe that Jesus Christ was the best, the holiest Man who ever lived?"—he is obliged to listen. You cannot expect a man to accept an abstract proposition that the Bible is the Word of God; that is not the first thing to bring before him. The first thing is: "What about Jesus Christ? If He was the best, the holiest Man who ever lived, He was the least likely to be deceived about Himself or to tell a lie. Then will you ask for what He says God will give—that is, the Holy Spirit?" A man ceases to be an honest doubter the moment he refuses one way of getting at the truth because he does not like that way.

The apostle Peter, when he preached to the Gentiles, spoke of Jesus not as the Son of God but as "Jesus of Nazareth, a man attested by God." That reveals the way in which the Holy Spirit brought Jesus Christ onto the platform on which men lived, and we have to do the same today. We have to be so controlled by the Holy Spirit, to so submit our intelligence to Him, that Jesus Christ is presented along the line that appeals to those to whom we talk.

Prejudice. "How can you believe, who receive honor from one another, and do not seek the honor that comes from the only God?" (John 5:44).

These words of Jesus bring out the very essence of prejudice—that is, to foreclose judgment without sufficiently weighing the evidence. "It is a moral impossibility for you to believe in Me," Jesus says in effect, "not because you are bad, but because you have another standard in view: you seek honor one of another." Remember, we see only along the line of our prejudice, and prejudice means ignorance. We are always prejudiced over what we know least about, and we foreclose our judgment about it. "I have sealed the question, docketed it, and put it into a pigeon-hole, and I refuse to say anything more about it" (see John 9:22). Then it is impossible for you to see along any other line until you are willing to take the packet out of the pigeon-hole, unseal it, and open the question again. Every point of view that I hold strongly makes me prejudiced, and I can see nothing else but that point of view. There is a ban of finality about it that makes me intolerant of any other point of view.

Up to the time of the resurrection, the disciples saw only along the line of their old narrow Jewish prejudices. When they received the Holy Spirit from the risen Lord, the operation performed on the inside enabled them to see along the line of Christ's revelation (see Luke 24:31, 45). What takes place at the new birth is an explosion on the inside (a literal explosion, not a theoretical one) that opens all the doors that have been closed. Life becomes larger; there is the incoming of a totally new point of view.

The way a searchlight works is a very good illustration for prejudice. A searchlight illumines only so much and no more; but let daylight come, and you find a thousand and one things the searchlight did not reveal. Whenever you get the light of God on salvation, it acts like a searchlight. Everything you read in the Bible teaches salvation and you say, "Why, it's as simple as can be!" The same with sanctification and the second coming. When you come to the place where God is the dominant light, you find facts you never realized before—facts no one is sufficient to explain except the Lord Jesus Christ.

Christianity is not walking in the light of our convictions, but walking in the light of the Lord, a very different thing. Convictions are necessary, but only as stepping stones to all that God wants us to be. The apostle Paul puts it in 1 Corinthians 4:3-4: "But with me it is a very small thing that I should be judged by you, or by a human court. In fact, I do not even judge myself. For I know nothing against myself, yet I am not justified by this; but He who judges me is the Lord." We have to get into the white light of Jesus Christ where He is easily first—not our experience of Him first, but Jesus Christ Himself first, and our experience the evidence that we have seen Him.

Doctrinal Difficulties

Distortions. "You search the Scriptures, for in them you think you have eternal life . . . but you are not willing to come to me that you may have life" (John 5:39-40).

These verses reveal how a knowledge of the Scriptures may distract the mind away from Jesus Christ. Unless we first know the Living Word personally, the literal words may lead us astray. The only way we can understand the Bible is by personal contact with the Living Word; then the Holy Spirit expounds the literal words to us along the line of personal experience. "The words I speak to you, they are spirit and they are life."

The Jews knew the Scriptures thoroughly, yet their minds were so distorted that when they saw Jesus Christ they said, "He has a demon." There is a context to the Bible, and that context is Jesus Christ. The right order is personal relationship to Him first, then the interpretation of the Scriptures according to His Spirit. Difficulties come because beliefs and creeds are put in the place of Jesus Christ.

Direction by Belief. "For many walk, of whom I have told you often, and now tell you even weeping, that they are the enemies of the cross of Christ . . ." (Philippians 3:18; see Colossians 2:8, 18-23).

Who are the enemies of the cross of Christ? First of all, what was the cross of Christ to Paul? The cross of a martyr? No. The cross to Paul was the cross of God whereby He readjusted humanity to Himself. "But God forbid that I should glory except in the cross of our Lord Jesus Christ, by whom the world has been crucified to me, and I to the world" (Galatians 6:14). "If any one preaches ordinances, the precepts and doctrines of men, and ignores the cross," Paul says, "I tell you even weeping, that they are the enemies of the revelation that God gave through Jesus Christ."

You can always detect the right kind of belief by a flesh-and-blood testimony. How many of us can say, "The life which I now live in the flesh"—the life you know and see—"I live by the faith of the Son of God"? Christian doctrines are the explanation of how Jesus Christ makes us saints; but all the doctrine under heaven will never make a saint. The only thing that will make a saint is the Holy Spirit working in us what Jesus Christ did in the atonement.

Jesus Christ demands absolute devotion to Himself personally, and then the application of His principles to our lives. For what purpose? That we may understand Him better. To be devoted to doctrines will twist us away from the center; devotion to Jesus Christ relates our doctrines to the one center—Jesus Christ. Read the words of the Spirit to the church in Ephesus: "Nevertheless I have this against you, that you left your first love." The doctrines you teach may be all right, but not if they are not centered in love for Jesus. "Remember therefore from where you have fallen; repent and do the first works" (Revelation 2:5).

Am I prepared to accept Jesus Christ's view of Himself, or have I a point of view? Will I come to Jesus Christ just as I am and face the fact that He says certain astounding things about Himself? Jesus Christ did not preach a gospel of hope; He came to reorganize humanity from the inside through a tremendous tragedy in His own life called the cross, and through that cross every member of the human race can be reinstated in God's favor and enter into a conscious inheritance of the atonement.

Jesus Christ is the only medium God almighty has for revealing Himself: "And no man knows the Father except the Son . . . ." Our Lord knows nothing about God being revealed in nature, in the love of our friends, etc. The poet talks about God being revealed in nature, but the poet does not remember that there is sin in the world. He sees clearly what God's idea is for man, but he forgets that we belong to a fallen race. Consequently, his poetry is only a vision; it cannot be worked out on Mother Earth.

"And he to whom the Son wills to reveal him" (Matthew 11:27). Who are the ones to whom Jesus Christ will reveal God? Jesus Christ will reveal God to all who come to Him—not those who accept certain creeds or doctrines, but those who come to Him, with beliefs or without them, if they will only get straight through to Him. "Come to Me, all you who labor and are heavy laden, and I will give you rest." "And the one who comes to Me I will by no means cast out."

Our Lord's View of Himself and His Work—II

The Force of the Fact of Christ on Thinking and Living

It is a tremendous thing to know that there are higher heights than we can scale, deeper depths than we can fathom. The reason average Christian workers remain average Christian workers is that they are grossly ignorant about things for which they see no immediate use. The majority of us are brought up on spooned meat: "For though by this time you ought to be teachers, you need someone to teach you again the first principles of the oracles of God; and you have come to need milk and not solid food" (Hebrews 5:12).

Method of Christian Thinking

Let this mind be in you which was also in Christ Jesus (Philippians 2:5).

The method of thinking for a Christian is first of all to become rightly related to Jesus Christ, and then to begin to think in accordance with His mind. There is nothing simple under heaven except the personal relationship to Jesus Christ, and Paul is concerned lest any philosophy should come in to corrupt the simplicity and purity that is toward

Christ, the simplicity of an understanding relationship between God and our own soul. "But I fear, lest somehow, as the serpent deceived Eve by his craftiness, so your minds may be corrupted from the simplicity that is in Christ" (2 Corinthians 11:3).

Today any number of religious books set out to expound Jesus Christ from a philosophical point of view. They are entrancing and apparently helpful, but in reality they do a great deal of harm, because instead of helping us to form the mind of Christ and understand His point of view, they serve to confuse our mind. When people ask for the "simple gospel" to be preached, they generally mean, "Preach us the thing we have always listened to, the thing that keeps us sound asleep. Don't present us with anything new." That means the mind is not open to accept facts, not open to entering into a relationship with God.

The cross is the symbol of Christian living and it is also the symbol of Christian thinking. Until a man is born again, his thinking goes round and round in a circle and he becomes intoxicated with his own importance. When he is born again, there is a violent readjustment in his actual life, and when he begins to think along Jesus Christ's line, there is just as tremendous a revolution in his thinking processes. To ignore the cross in either living or thinking is to become a traitor to Jesus Christ.

The apostle Paul tells us how our thinking as saints is to be conducted—by "casting down imaginations [reasonings], and every high thing that is exalted against the knowledge of God, and bringing every thought into captivity to the obedience of Christ."

To bring every thought into captivity is the last thing we do, and it is not done easily. In the beginning we have to do violence to our old ways of thinking, just as at sanctification we had to do violence to our old ways of living. Intellect in a saint is the last thing to become identified with Jesus Christ. Paul urges, "Let this mind be in you which was also in Christ Jesus." Many a Christian who loves Jesus Christ in his heart denies Him in his head.

The method of thinking for the saint is not to think along the line of Christian principles, but after he has become rightly related to Jesus Christ to see that he allows nothing to corrupt the profound simplicity of that relationship. That will mean we will have only those experiences that Jesus Christ sanctions. If you go on the line of accepting whatever can be experienced, you will find you have to accept the wildest, vaguest, most indeterminate things.

For example, a man may come and tell you that he has had communication with departed friends. Well, he is no more likely to be untruthful than you are. How are you going to judge whether his experience is right or not? The only guide is your personal relationship to Jesus Christ. Jesus Christ prohibits it, and that shuts the door straight off from your tampering with spiritualism. Therefore, you refuse to have anything to do with what He will not allow.

It is imperative to estimate the danger abroad today in books that deal with Christian thinking, particularly those which have the word psychology tacked on. Be sure what kind of psychology it is; unless it is the psychology of the Bible, it may be the psychology of agnosticism pure and simple. It may sound all right but in the final result it dethrones Jesus Christ.

The Christian method of thinking has its source in a personal relationship to Jesus Christ, and this means we have to take into account our Lord's view of Himself. As you read the New Testament, the first thing that strikes you with overwhelming clarity is that our Lord's fundamental view of Himself was His oneness with the Father. The first and foremost consciousness of Jesus was not the needs of mankind, not the pitiable condition of people, but His relationship to His Father whose name He had to hallow before all else.

Our Lord's holy living was produced by submitting Himself to His Father: "Most assuredly, I say to you, the Son can do nothing of Himself, but what He sees the Father do" (John 5:19). His holy speaking was produced by submitting His intellect to His Father. "For I have not spoken on my own authority; but the Father who sent Me, gave me a command, what I should say, and what I should speak" (John 12:49). And His holy miracle-working was produced by submitting His will to His Father: "The Father who dwells in Me does the works" (John 14:10).

That is our Lord's view of Himself, and when we become identified with Him He relates us to Himself as He was related to His Father " . . . that they may be one, even as We are." As saints, are we submitting our intellect to the revealed will of God and refusing to be corrupted from the simplicity of that relationship? The insistence all through the epistles is on being "transformed by the renewing of your mind," on having our minds "stirred up by being put in remembrance," and on "building ourselves up on our most holy faith." We are called upon to be right not only in heart, but in thinking. When we have become personally related to Jesus Christ, we have to do the thing that is in our power to do—that is, to think rightly.

In Philippians 4:8-9 Paul gives the rule for the thinking life of the Christian. Have we ever given our brains the task of concentrated thinking along this line? "Finally, brethren, whatever things are true, whatever things are noble, whatever things are just, whatever things are pure, whatever things are lovely, whatever things are of good report; if there is any virtue and if there is anything praiseworthy, think on these things." It is because we will not bring every thought into captivity to the obedience of Christ that all the perplexities are produced regarding methods of thinking that look like Christianity. Strands are taken out of Jesus Christ's teaching, the Bible is exploited to agree with certain principles, but the Truth, our Lord Jesus, Christ is ignored.

If we base our thinking on principles instead of on a Person we shall go wrong, no matter how devout or honest we are. The one great truth to keep steadfastly before us is the Lord Jesus Christ; He is the Truth. Only the whole truth is the truth; any part of the truth may become an error. If you have a ray of light on the truth, never call it the whole truth; follow it up and it will lead you to the central Truth, the Lord Jesus Christ.

Method of Christian Living

> For to this you were called, because Christ also suffered for us, leaving us an example, that you should follow His steps ... (1 Peter 2:21).

The life of a Christian is stamped by a strong family likeness to Jesus. When we become rightly related to God on the ground of the redemption, our brains have to begin to think along the lines Jesus Christ thought on, and in our bodily life there will be produced a likeness to Him, so that people will "realize that we have been with Jesus." The piety not built on a personal relationship to Jesus Christ is simply religious egotism, and the dislike that most of us have against pious people is wholesomely right.

A pious person is simply overweeningly conceited religiously; he substitutes prayer and consecration for devotion to Jesus: "I am going to give so much time to prayer, so much time to Bible study, and by doing these things I shall produce the kind of life that will please God." Where does Jesus Christ come in? He does not come in anywhere. The first thing the Holy Spirit does is to take away all sense of our own importance and to produce in us a state of true humility.

The test of all doctrine is, Does it produce a likeness to Jesus Christ? The final test is how a man's thinking works out in his life. The apostle Paul warns against thinking that by sheer willpower a man can do what he likes: "These things indeed have an appearance of wisdom in self-imposed religion . . . but are of no value against the indulgence of the flesh" (Colossians 2:23). The test of this "will to power" method of thinking is, Does it have any element of power over the wrong thing, over the disposition of sin? Jesus Christ alone can deal with that.

Take another method of thinking, the aesthetic—and here I am on the ground that I know better than any other, except my soul's salvation. An aesthete bases all his thinking on the principle that anything that produces joy is justifiable for him. Aestheticism may be all very well for the kingdom of heaven, but it is the doctrine of the devil himself for the kingdom of earth. If once you base your thinking on the principles of aestheticism, you can justify any kind of vile corruption.

The test of every system of thinking is not how it works in the best case, but how it works in the worst case. If the test were the best cases—that is, if everyone were well brought up, if men and women did not have a moral twist—then any of these philosophies would work out quite well. The miracle of the redemption of Jesus Christ is that He can take the worst and the vilest of men and women and make saints out of them.

Another method of thinking is egoistical. The egoist is one who centers all his thinking around human personality. The number of books written from this standpoint is legion. "Our greatest work," they say, "is to get straight down to the one important thing—man, his dignity and nobility— and to look after his needs." What is the practical outworking of this? That God and man are one and the same. All we have to do is to let our inmost personality have expression—and what are we doing? We are expressing God. Is that line of thinking unfamiliar today? It is becoming more and more familiar.

The Christian method of thinking puts the intellect second, not first; the modern view puts intellect on the throne. God does not sum up a person's worth by his thinking, but by the way he expresses his thinking in actual life—that is, by his character. It is possible for there to be a tremendous divorce between a man's thinking and his practical life; the only thing that tells in the sight of God is a man's character. Beware of putting principles first instead of a Person. Jesus Christ puts personal relationship first: "Be rightly related to Me, then work out your thinking."

In these methods of thinking that contrast with the Christian method, certain aspects of Christianity are stressed while other aspects are ignored, and in this way people's minds are corrupted from the simplicity that is in Christ Jesus. The presentation given of Jesus Christ in these methods of thinking is of one who has a little more breath than the rest of us; He is in the same "swim," but able to turn around and give us a helping hand.

Is this the New Testament view of Jesus Christ? Jesus

said, "Upon this rock I will build my Church"—the rock of personal revelation of who Jesus Christ is, "The Son of the living God." This is the invincible fact against which nothing can prevail. Along this line we see the profundity of the apostle Paul's words "For I determined not to know anything among you except Jesus Christ, and Him crucified" (1 Corinthians 2:2).

According to the New Testament, the historic Jesus and the eternal Christ are one and the same. The glorified Lord who appeared to Paul in all His ascended majesty is "this same Jesus" who "trod this earth with naked feet, and wove with human hands the creed of creeds." The Jesus who saves our souls and identifies us with Himself is "this same Jesus" who went to sleep as a baby on His mother's bosom; and it is "this same Jesus," the almighty, powerful Christ, with all power in heaven and on earth, who is at work in the world today by His Spirit.

Our Lord's View of Himself and His Work—III

The Finality of the Person of Jesus Christ

Finality means there is nothing to be added. In our previous studies we have been clearing the ground for studying the Person of our Lord Jesus Christ, and warning ourselves of the danger of bringing to that study a mental point of view that we have no right to bring. We must be prepared to accept facts and not try to build facts into our preconceived fancies.

"The Word became flesh . . ." What Word? The explaining Word about God, about creation, about man, became incarnate, a flesh-and-blood fact, and trod this earth with human feet, and worked with human hands, and thought with a human brain. Now perplexities and fogs have gone forever! The Bible never asks us to try and find out God. The human mind can never work along that line. The Bible is dictated by the Holy Spirit and He knows exactly the lines along which human minds can work.

"All things have been delivered to me by My Father; and no one knows the Son except the Father. Nor does anyone know the Father except the Son, and he to whom the Son wills to reveal Him" (Matthew 11:27). Every other line of finding out God is atheistic impertinence, and trying to think about man is presumption, as long as we ignore the one fact we can find out, the Lord Jesus Christ, and the interpreting fact about Him, which is the Bible.

The Original Position of Man
Genesis 2:7; Romans 5:12

When we read that "the Lord God formed man of the dust of the ground," remember that man was the federal head of the race—not man as a member of the degenerate race to which we belong, but man as he came direct from the hand of God—and "breathed into his nostrils the breath of life; and man became a living being." God breathed into man that which, going forth from God and entering into man, became the spirit of man. That spirit is essentially man's spirit, and never ceases to be man's spirit. This is an insistent revelation all through the Bible.

In John 20:22 another "breathing" is mentioned. After the resurrection, Jesus "breathed on them and said to them, 'Receive the Holy Spirit.' " The human spirit thus became energized by the Spirit of the Son of God. We must keep this distinction in mind in order to understand the difference between Christian belief and the beliefs of other religions, which are spreading all over our land—that is, that the human spirit is simply a drop whipped out of the ocean of God's Spirit, that individuality is a mistake, and that man is going to drop back again into God's Being and cease to be. The points of view are fundamentally different. Man's spirit is as immortal as God's Spirit; God can no more annihilate man's spirit than He can annihilate Himself.

Soul is the expression of spirit in the body; soul has no existence apart from spirit and body. As soon as body goes, the spirit returns to God who gave it, and soul is not. The resurrection is of body, not of spirit or soul. Spirit is the immortal, indestructible part of a man, and it goes back to God who gave it, with all the characteristics that marked it while it was on earth. When the Bible speaks of the resurrection body of a good man, it says it is to be like Jesus Christ's glorious body (Philippians 3:21). Our Lord does not give the picture of the resurrection body of a bad man, but He does say there will be a "resurrection of condemnation" (John 5:29).

The fundamental basis of the life of mankind was the life of God and communion with God, and until he fell, Adam's spirit and soul and body were in absolute harmony with God. What do we mean by the Fall? God intended man to progress from innocence to holiness by a series of deliberate moral choices in which he was to sacrifice the life of nature to the will of God. Adam refused to do this, and that constitutes the Fall.

When Adam fell the Spirit of God was withdrawn instantly, not after a time. The real seat of death is in a person's spirit; the dissolution of the body is a mere incident. The point God's Book emphasizes is the instant withdrawal of life, the withdrawal of the Spirit that held man's spirit, soul, and body in living communion with God. "Therefore, just as through one man sin entered the world, and death through sin, and thus death spread to all men, because all have sinned" (Romans 5:12).

Up until the Fall, man drew all his sustenance from God; when he fell, he lost that harmony completely. And the danger now is that although man's spirit is as immortal as God's, it receives no sustenance from God. The first thing that happened was that man became his own god—exactly what the devil said would happen. Read Genesis 3 and you will find what the devil insinuates: "God knows that if you eat of the fruit of the tree, and take the rule of yourself into your own hands, you will become as He is." And verse 22 is the confirmation from God's standpoint that man has become as He is: "Behold, the man has become like one of us, to know good and evil." Man obliterated God from the throne and claimed that he was god. That is the essential principle of sin—"my claim to my right to myself." Insubordination is the characteristic of the fallen spirit of man; he will not sacrifice the natural life for the spiritual.

Personality, which in the Bible is synonymous with spirit, reveals itself in bodily life more or less clearly. The Spirit of God alone knows the full limit of our personality. The psalmist's attitude, therefore, is the right one: "Search me, O God; I am too deep to understand myself." Unless I have received the Holy Spirit, my personality is dead to all God has to say. I have no affinity with anything God wants; I am my own god. But through the atonement I can receive the Holy Spirit, who imparts to me the life of Jesus, and I am lifted into the domain where He is, and by obedience I can be led to the place of identification with His death.

Soul in fallen man is the expression of his personality, either in morality or in immorality. When Jesus Christ judges people He judges them according to the spirit, not according to soul—that is, the fleshly presentation of their personality. He saw what we do not see: the spirit behind. The spirit of fallen man does not have the life of God in it; it has no power within it to discern God (see 1 Corinthians 2:10-14). The meaning of the atonement is that the human spirit can be restored into harmony with God. It is not human nature that needs altering; it is man's spirit that needs to be brought back into right relationship with God. And before that can be done, the disposition of sin has to be dealt with.

The gift of God to every fallen son of Adam is the gift of the Holy Spirit—that is, the essential power and nature of God coming into a man and lifting him to a totally new Kingdom. That power can be had for the asking: "If you then, being evil, know how to give good gifts to your children, how much more shall your heavenly Father give the Holy Spirit to those who ask Him?" (Luke 11:13). Yet is it not strange that people should go through seas of trouble before they get to the length of asking? If a man says, "I have this power in myself, and all that is necessary is to develop it," then he will never be in agreement with Jesus Christ. Jesus says, "You have not [this] life in yourselves." The Fall obliterated it entirely; the gift of life was withdrawn and "death reigned."

Death is not annihilation; we exist in a kingdom of death (see Ephesians 2:1). In the Bible the term "life" is used only of the life of God. Man lives—to use a seeming contradiction of terms—in the kingdom of death, and only when he is born from above by the Holy Spirit does he enter into the kingdom of life (John 3:3). When man is right with God he is filled with God's Spirit. Whenever Jesus speaks about life He is referring to the life that is in Himself, and it is this life that He imparts by means of His death.

The Original Position of Jesus Christ

And now, O Father, glorify Me together with Yourself, with the glory which I had with You before the world was (John 17:5).

In these words the essence of the personality of Jesus is made known; it is identified as being exactly the same as almighty God's. The snare of the modern tendency is in saying that we can know all about Jesus Christ if we will simply examine ourselves; Jesus says we cannot: "No one knows the Son except the Father . . . ."

Jesus Christ makes the distinction perfectly clear between His personality and our human personalities. Jesus Christ had a twofold personality: He was Son of God revealing what God is like, and Son of Man revealing what man is to be like. When our Lord talks about His own personality, He identifies Himself with God almighty: "I and my Father are one." For any man to say that would be blasphemy; we are not one with almighty God. But through the atonement we become one with Jesus Christ, and He brings us into union with God: ". . . that they may be one as We are." That is the meaning of the atonement—the at-one-ment.

"Who, being in the form of God . . . made Himself of no reputation . . . coming in the likeness of man." Our Lord might have taken the form of an angel (Hebrews 2:10), but He could not take the form of anything lower than man, because man is the last reach of creation in the image of God. Angels belong to a different realm; man was made in the likeness of God (see Genesis 1:26). In the incarnation Jesus Christ came down to the lowest rung possible; He came on to where Adam was originally, and He lived on that plane in order to show what God's normal man was like. And then He did what no man could ever do; He made the way for man to get back to the position he had lost. By the sheer might of the atonement we can be reinstated in God's favor; that is the marvel.

After we are identified with the death of Jesus, the life of Jesus becomes the pattern for our walk in this world. Jesus Christ transformed innocence into holiness by sacrificing Himself to God. When we are rightly related to God, the golden rule for our life is the sacrifice of our wills to Jesus Christ. It has to be submission of the intellect all along the line, and in these mortal bodies of ours, impaired and damaged through sin though they are, we are to manifest the life of Jesus. The same body that used to be the seat of a soul expressing the wrong disposition can make itself the seat of a soul expressing a strong family likeness to Jesus.

The sacrifice of Jesus is the essence of renunciation. It was "a sacrifice to God for a sweet smelling savor." The death of Jesus was not a satisfaction paid to the justice of God—a hideous statement that the Bible nowhere makes. The death of Jesus was an exact revelation of the justice of God. When we read of the sacrifice of Jesus Christ, it is the sacrifice of God also. ". . . . God was in Christ reconciling the world to Himself." When Jesus Christ lifts the veil from His own consciousness, He makes it clear that His death was not the death of a martyr. "I lay down my life of myself. I have power to lay it down, and I have power to take it again." Our Lord laid down His life for one purpose, the express purpose in the mind of God: He is "the Lamb of God, who takes away the sin of the world," "the Lamb slain from the foundation of the world."

There is nothing obscure about these revelations, but they are so deep that only the Holy Spirit can reveal them. Where are we with regard to understanding these mysteries of our faith? Along with the craving to be right with God, there is also a deep resentment, born of our laziness, that we should be expected to understand these things. But the urgency all through the New Testament is that we should stir up our minds to search out these things, and build ourselves up on our most holy faith. We are called upon not only to be right in heart, but to be right in thinking.

Note to the Reader

The publisher invites you to share your response to the message of this book by writing Discovery House Publishers, P.O. Box 3566, Grand Rapids, MI 49501, U.S.A. or by calling 1-800-283-8333. For information about other Discovery House publications, contact us at the same address and phone number.

My Utmost for His Highest
by *Oswald Chambers*
     The classic devotional bestseller. These powerful words will refresh those who need encouragement, brighten the way of those in difficulty, and strengthen personal relationships with Christ. A book to use every day for the rest of your life.

Audio Tape Edition: The complete work on twelve cassettes.

The Oswald Chambers Library
     Powerful insights on topics of interest to every believer:

If You Will Ask
     Reflections on the power of prayer.

The Love of God
     An intimate look at the Father-heart of God.

The Place of Help
     Thoughts on daily needs of the Christian life.

Not Knowing Where
     Keen spiritual direction through knowing and trusting God.

Baffled to Fight Better
     Job and the problem of suffering.

Order from your favorite bookstore or from:

DISCOVERY HOUSE PUBLISHERS
Box 3566
Grand Rapids, MI 49501
Call toll-free: 1-800-283-8333